"BECAUSE I'm
THE MOTHER
That's WHY!"

"Because I'm the Mother That's Why!"

---o---

Mostly True Confessions of Modern Motherhood

By STEPHANIE PIERSON

Illustrations by Mary Lynn Blasutta

Delacorte Press

Published by
Delacorte Press
Bantam Doubleday Dell Publishing Group, Inc.
1540 Broadway
New York, New York 10036

Library of Congress Cataloging in Publication Data
Pierson, Stephanie.
"Because I'm the mother, that's why!": mostly true confessions of
modern motherhood / by Stephanie Pierson ; illustrations by Mary
Lynn Blasutta.
p. cm.
ISBN 0-385-31096-X
1. Pierson, Stephanie. 2. Mothers — New York (State) — Anecdotes.
I. Title.
HQ759.P53A3 1994

306.874'3 — dc20   93-5917
                                                                  CIP

Manufactured in the United States of America
Published simultaneously in Canada

May 1994

10 9 8 7 6 5 4 3 2 1
RRH

To Megan Connell. For being beautiful, talented, and kind, and for sharing her dad.

Love and gratitude to Bob Gouveia, Jackie Cantor, Emily Reichert, Michael Cader, Dian Ohrnberger, Dorothy Kalins, Helene Newman, Enid Armstrong, Dylan Jones. And to Gordon Fenton: Sage, Savant, Raconteur, Philosopher, Beloved Boss.

CONTENTS

Many, many people envy the life I lead, and who could blame them? I have a husband who has come home every night since 1981, a ten-year-old who only occasionally calls me by the housekeeper's name, a full-time job, two zip codes, a dog who licks my inner ear when he's anxious, and more bills than just about anyone I know.

Now and then I like to sit back and take stock of the rich cornucopia that's my life. My husband is too busy playing Tetris on his computer to look at other women. The dog is beyond hope. I still have my job because, I suppose, nobody else wants it. So the bulk of my time is spent trying to raise my daughter, Phoebe, with love, care, and the occasional bribe.

Now that Phoebe's ten, I know what I've done *for* her. Unfortunately I think it's going to be years before I know what I've done *to* her.

How much will she blame me for what happened in her formative years? Will she remember the time I accidentally dropped the Fisher-Price Chime Ball on her head? Did she overhear me telling Daddy that if she made me do that "Orange you glad I didn't say banana?" knock-knock joke one more time, I was going to kill myself? Will she hold it against me that I don't know who wrote the book of love, who put the bop in the bop-sh-bop-sh-bop, or why fools fall in love? Will she understand that the reason I couldn't explain what extra-virgin olive oil is is because she didn't know what a virgin is?

Personally I know I've given Phoebe all the unconditional love and emotional tools she needs to grow up to be another Margaret Thatcher, Joan of Arc, or Janet Reno.

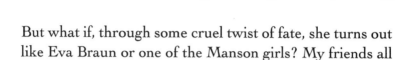

But what if, through some cruel twist of fate, she turns out like Eva Braun or one of the Manson girls? My friends all tell me what a good job I'm doing, but I bet Joan Crawford's friends told her the same thing.

I picture Phoebe on "Oprah" with millions of shocked viewers watching as she calmly explains why matricide was the only option. Why a small voice inside her kept saying, "It was Mommy." But maybe I shouldn't worry so much. A couple of weeks ago Phoebe actually kissed me on the lips. Just the other day she said to me, "Mom, I hate Daddy much more than I hate you." She can't work a gun, our kitchen knives are never sharp, and it's been months since she's asked to rent that movie about the kid who divorces his parents.

So I guess I'm not doing so badly. Here's to dull knives, sharp kids, and bright futures. Because I said so. Because I love you. Because I'm the mother, that's why.

1

It's a

Girl!

THROW BABY ON THE TRAIN
Phoebe Is Five

First I got an apartment in the city. Then I got a husband in the city. Then we got a house in the country. Then we got a Subaru station wagon to take us there. Then we got a baby to take with us. So far so good. Then the husband in the city found that his job with the opera left him lots of time to spend in the country. He got to take the Subaru. I got to take the enchanting five-year-old child on the commuter train with me.

Oh, said my husband, you'll have fun. Kids love trains.

Remember when commuting meant: take a train, take a newspaper, take a beer take a nap? These days the trip breaks down somewhat differently:

5:10 P.M. — Meet Phoebe and beloved housekeeper at information booth at Grand Central.

5:11 P.M. — Race to Zaro's. Buy one Day-Glo punch and one chemical carrot cake for train.

5:15 P.M. — Kiss beloved housekeeper good-bye fifty-two times and get on train.

5:16 P.M. — Sit down in empty seat. Start taking objects out of Phoebe's tote bag for Fun on Train.

5:20 P.M. — Give Phoebe punch to drink. Top not on tight. Punch spills.

5:21 P.M. — Clean punch off Phoebe's T-shirt. Root around for clean shirt. Give her carrot cake. Tuck many napkins in clean shirt. Pick up *Newsweek*.

5:23 P.M. — Give ticket to conductor. Conductor gives bunch of old ticket stubs to Phoebe to play with. Phoebe, in an excess of zeal, grabs stubs and glops carrot cake (orange) all over my silk skirt (white). Give Phoebe short lecture about grabbing and cost of dry cleaning. Suggest Phoebe look at scenery.

5:23½ P.M. — Scenery boring. Read *One Fish, Two Fish, Red Fish, Blue Fish.*

5:30 P.M. — Give Phoebe markers and "Sesame Street" coloring book. Suggest that Miss Piggy's dress should be red. Pick up *Newsweek.*

5:35 P.M. — Wonder why seat feels lumpy. (Am sitting on four markers.) Try to get marker stain (green) off silk skirt (white and chemical orange). Vexed with Phoebe. Phoebe vexed with me for sitting on her best markers.

5:45 P.M. — Phoebe has to go to bathroom "right now" and she feels sick riding backward and why am I always reading that stupid magazine instead of paying attention to her?

5:46 P.M. — Take Phoebe to filthy bathroom. Wash hands. Detach wet toilet paper from soles of her sneakers. Lurch back to seat.

6 P.M. — Give Phoebe Fisher-Price Cookie Counter to play with. Pick up *Newsweek.* Phoebe wants to

know: What's 9 minus 44, what's 10 plus 111, what comes after 99, and why?

6:15 P.M. — Play game called What's the Yuckiest Thing in the Whole World for Dinner? The winner is chocolate-covered ants topped with hair and thumbtacks. The runner-up is octopus eyes with graham crackers.

6:25 P.M. — Count sleeping commuters. Count swans on lake outside of train. Count how long it will be until we get there. Fantasize about martinis. Tell Phoebe to stop kicking me. Phoebe says she can't help it, my knees are in her way. Move over two inches.

6:30 P.M. — Conductor announces Brewster. Spirits soar. Retrieve Phoebe's toys, markers, books, games, and so on, from seat and floor. Race to door.

6:33 P.M. — Stagger up steps of station and look for Daddy in parking lot. Many kisses and hugs. Phoebe tells Daddy that all Mommy did on train was read magazine and kick her. On purpose! Drive home. Stop at liquor store. Have a wonderful weekend.

—%—%—%—

LIVING WITH A SUPERJOCK
Phoebe Is Five

 My idea of strenuous exercise is going through the sale racks at Bergdorf's or carrying home four bottles of Perrier from Sloan's. There's only one other form of exercise I heartily endorse, and I'm happy to say I got great results to show for it: a six-pound, eleven-ounce baby girl.

A girl! My fantasies come true! A sweet, docile child I could dress in Liberty pinafores, who would sit quietly with me as we leafed through the pages of *Alice's Adventures in Wonderland*, who would teach herself petit point, who would spend hours arranging the miniature wicker furniture in her antique dollhouse.

Like mother, like daughter, I had been led to believe. The apple doesn't fall far from the tree, I had always been told. A chip off the old block, I think the expression goes. I can't bear to go on. Of course in one of life's little ironic twists, some dimly recessive gene surfaced from the family pool to produce the biggest female jock this side of steroid-stuffed Romanian discus throwers. We named her Phoebe, Greek for "light." We should have named her Sluggo, English for "Get a load of those pecs!"

At eight months Phoebe could walk. At fifteen months Phoebe could climb to the top of the jungle gym and vault down. At thirty-three months Phoebe was roller-skating half a mile every day to nursery school. At four years Phoebe was going up chair lifts and skiing down the intermediate slopes.

At age five Phoebe has a room that looks like the New York branch of Gold's Gym: soccer balls, tennis balls, baseballs, Wiffle balls, Nerf balls, basketballs. A bowling set, a basketball set, a soccer set. Roller skates, ice skates, a small Flexible Flyer, downhill skis, cross-country skis. A two-wheeler, an old tricycle, badminton rackets, tennis rackets, a trampoline, and a skateboard.

If life were fair, extremely active children like Phoebe would all be born in Wyoming, where there are zillions of miles of empty space to bounce around in and wild horses to ride and large mountains to climb. Maybe God didn't know we live in a six-room apartment deep in the heart of Manhattan.

Go anywhere outside of New York City and you'll hear others calling to their children, "Go out and play in the yard, dear!" and "Please take that soccer ball into the rumpus room right now!" and "If you want to practice riding your tricycle, Daddy will put it out on the patio." Words like *rumpus room, patio*, and *backyard* bring tears to my eyes. Don't even mention *finished basement, attic,* or *swimming pool*. Our recreational facilities are so small that the very same Frisbee throw that knocked over and broke the Steuben vase ricocheted off the coffee table and broke the glass on the David Hockney poster. Try that in Wyoming!

But thanks to a refillable prescription for 5 milligrams of Valium (for me) and some careful planning (for Phoebe), we have managed to bring up our little Nadia Comaneci and still maintain a semblance of sanity. Our first investment for Phoebe was a good pair of running shoes ($20). Our second was a country house ($200,000). This may seem a little steep, but so far it's been worth every thousand. Our ongoing Monday-to-Friday investments have included aforementioned sports equipment plus every class in town that offered a real workout for the child (and

where possible, a chance for the mother to spend the class time at the coffee shop on the corner).

Phoebe has attended gymnastics classes, swim classes, ballet classes, and run-them-ragged summer camps.

When we were looking at nursery schools, we were less interested in how many colors of Play-Doh were available than in whether or not they had lots of space, a large gym, and a park right across the street. Phoebe's off to kindergarten in the fall, and we think she's going to love it. Her new school has three gyms! A dance program! Volleyball! Gymnastics! A swim team! Track! Tennis! Squash! It even has great academics in case she has time. Her new school goes all the way from kindergarten to high school. As far as college, who knows? Do you think that Texas A&M scouts Brearley?

−%−%−%−

RAISING BETTY CROCKER
Phoebe Is Six

My great-grandmother was a seamstress nonpareil. She sewed for a living and in her spare time dressed me in ensembles that suggested a cross between Beatrix Potter and Prince Albert. My grandmother was a born cook: savory Swedish pot roasts, homemade lingonberry sauce, a creamy rice pudding to die from (my great-grandmother did actually die right after eating this rice pudding one New Year's Eve, but that's another story). My mother is a master knitter: intricate cable-knit sweaters, enchanting baby bootees, and argyle vests festooned with marching Scotties.

So, quelle surprise: My inheritance in this domestic gene pool is zilch. I don't cook, I don't knit, I don't bake, I don't crochet, I don't sew. My rule of thumb is: If one button is missing, wear it anyway. If two buttons are missing, throw it out. Two weeks ago I tried cooking Jerusalem artichokes for my husband. After three and one-half hours of serious boiling, the vegetables were rock-hard and I discovered that I was cooking gingerroot instead.

I learned to live a normal life with what I like to think of as my domestic handicap. We order out Chinese. I Scotch-tape my hems. My husband orders Jerusalem artichokes in restaurants. And life would have proceeded apace if I hadn't happened to give birth to a pint-size version of Betty Crocker.

Phoebe is now six. She loves to iron, sew buttons, bake, cook, clean, shop, wash dishes, make place cards, polish the silver, decorate her dollhouse, give pretend tea parties, make pot holders, sweep the floor with her tiny broom and dustpan, and scrub the kitchen counter. Somehow she got the role without the role model. She knows more about double coupons than I do. She sews buttons on my husband's shirts. She irons her own blouses.

At first, I have to admit it, I was devastated. "What's cooking, Mom? It smells good," Phoebe would say. "Stouffer's Macaroni and Cheese!" I would brightly reply. "What's that Scotch tape doing on your hem, Mom?" she would innocently ask. "Gosh, I have no idea, Phoebe." I would answer. "Can you help me finish this pot holder, Mom?" "Ask Daddy," I would riposte. By the time she was four, she had gotten the picture. "Mom doesn't know anything about this stuff, right, Dad?"

Everyone pitches in to compensate for me. My husband is teaching Phoebe to needlepoint. My mother is making dollhouse curtains. My sister-in-law fashions all of Phoebe's Halloween costumes. (Phoebe was crestfallen a few years ago when I told her, "If I can't *buy* it, you can't *be* it.") Thanks to our housekeeper, Phoebe can darn socks, use the delicate cycle, peel potatoes, and test the spaghetti to see if it's done.

Phoebe, mercifully, seems to be doing just fine without my help. We're doing fine too. My husband has buttons on all his shirts. There's always pepper in the pepper mill. The dishes don't stack up in the sink. When I reheat the mooshu pork, there's always a little pot holder handy. I like to think of myself as the only woman in America who married her husband and gave birth to a wife.

–%–%–%–

SHADES OF MY CHILDHOOD
Phoebe Is Seven

Nothing seems more all-American than making all-American icons disappear forever. My own personal bereavement list ranges from diners to cars with fins, from the Brooklyn Dodgers to Fiestaware, from the *Saturday Evening Post* to the Automat. And just when you thought it was safe to go back in the water, Crayola announced that for the first time in history, they were "retiring" eight classic crayon colors, and eight new Now and Wow colors were taking their place.

Crayola honored the departing colors with a ceremony at their headquarters in Easton, Pennsylvania. There was a farewell cake. A folk singer. Miss Pennsylvania was there too. She's a ventriloquist. She unveiled the five-foot replicas of each crayon to be enshrined forever in the hallowed Crayola Hall of Fame. So the good news is that these eight colors haven't entirely disappeared. The bad news is you have to go to Easton, Pennsylvania, to visit them.

All Americans were affected by Crayola's decision. Small Americans too. When I told Phoebe the news, she took it remarkably well. "It's okay, Mom, as long as they're keeping Lemon Yellow." How to break it to her? Of course they weren't keeping Lemon Yellow. Gorgeous, sunny, pure Lemon Yellow is gone, replaced by a vaguely neon shade called Dandelion. Not even a flower, a weed.

Ring out Maize, Raw Umber, Blue Gray, Green Blue, Violet Blue, Orange Red, and Orange Yellow. And ring in (besides the new weed color) Wild Strawberry, Vivid Tangerine, Fuchsia, Teal Blue, Royal Purple, Jungle Green, and Cerulean (a breeze for a three-year-old to pronounce).

And why is Crayola tampering with this American icon? Because market research has indicated that today's children prefer brighter, more vibrant colors. Well, I have a Today's Child who prefers Count Chocula cereal to Shredded Wheat, and I am not planning to reward this misguided preference with a major marketing shift that could alter history.

More to the point, is nothing sacred? Are these the same market researchers who recommended changing Coke's formula? What will Crayola do if tomorrow's children prefer duller colors? Is Burnt Sienna safe? Is Elvis really dead? Or is it me? I've wrestled long and hard with the possibility that I may have reached an age that simply resists change.

And I can honestly say I don't think that's it. After all, I was delighted when Oprah lost all that weight. I was pleased as punch when Joan Rivers got another face-lift. And I adjusted almost immediately to the new time slot for "The Simpsons."

So what is it? I guess it's the unforgivable crime of

tampering with my childhood. How many years did I spend coloring the ocean Green Blue? How many of Minnie's dresses had Orange Red polka dots? Huey, Dewey, and Louie's feathers were always Maize.

I'd say we'll adjust, but it isn't true. We won't. We don't have to. Right after Crayola's announcement I went out and bought ten sixty-four-color boxes, thereby assuring us a stockpile of old colors. So I'm happy to report that Lemon Yellow is alive and well at my house. And I'm a lot less cerulean than I was.

EXORCISING PHOEBE
Phoebe Is Eight

I never got to see the exorcism segment on "20/20" that everyone was talking about, but I heard about it and it sounded great! In fact my husband and I were so inspired by the whole thing that we've decided to do an exorcism on our eight-year-old daughter, Phoebe.

Phoebe's a terrific kid, but right now she's going through a terrible phase. She's been grumpy, whiny, moody, and temperamental — usually all at the same time.

If you heard some of the snippy things she says to us, it would make your head spin (whoops!).

We know it will pass, but our feeling is, why should we live through something that might last weeks or even months, when a quick exorcism could snap her right out of it? And who knows, maybe we could get a guest shot on "Geraldo" or at least a cover story in the *National Enquirer*. Phoebe *is* extremely photogenic, especially when she's got a lot of color in her face.

I don't know how specific you can get on this, but we'd really love it if the priest could exorcise certain words and phrases that keep spewing out of Phoebe's cherubic mouth, such as "Gimme!" "Now!" and "Make me!" There are whole sentences, too, that come out in a terrible, other-worldly voice, such as: "Everybody else's parents let *them*!" and "You expect me to eat something that looks like *that*?!" The other day I could swear I heard the Voice say, "My *real* parents would let me stay up and watch 'Beavis and Butt-head,'" but maybe I was just imagining that. We're all a little overwrought.

I don't know how much you can get accomplished in one session, but if there's time, we'd give anything to have the Nintendo demons driven out. Two solid hours of Super Mario and Phoebe has a good shot at winning the Linda Blair look-alike contest.

After the success of "20/20," it's probably harder to get an exorcism appointment than it is to get in to see Catherine

Deneuve's plastic surgeon, but believe me, we'll make ourselves available. Just about any school night is good, except for Wednesdays, when Phoebe gets home late from Brownies, and Thursdays, when she has her cello lesson.

We do have a couple of questions. First of all, we're not Catholic, although we must have watched *The Sound of Music* a million times and we can sing every note. And we'd like to know if the exorcism comes with any kind of guarantee. Frankly we're afraid that when Phoebe is a full-fledged teenager, she might need some remedial work. Our dog, Ollie, for example, sailed through his puppy-training classes, then totally forgot how to roll over, so he got a short refresher course, free.

Speaking of free, exactly how much does all this cost? We really only want a simple ceremony, just immediate family and some cold hors d'oeuvres. And does insurance cover any part of it? My husband's plan at work is excellent, although this seems like a fairly new area of coverage. Except maybe in southern California.

Of course the biggest question is what to wear. Right now I'm leaning toward something kind of casual but pulled together — maybe a DKNY jumpsuit or just black Gap leggings with a great white shirt and a silk scarf. Very little jewelry. I think it's just uncanny how Barbara Walters *always* has the appropriate outfit.

You don't jump into these things casually, and of course I do have a lot of anxiety. Will there be enough to eat? Does

white photograph well? How much do we tip? But I think the emotional toll an exorcism might take on me is worth it to get back Phoebe, my most precious possession. And I mean that literally.

CHILDHOOD QUOTES
Phoebe Is Ten

Me to Phoebe During Visit to the Vet, Age 2
"Phoebe, when you grow up, do you want to be a dog doctor?"
"Oh, no! When I grow up, I want to be the dog."

Phoebe Meeting the New Elevator Man, Age 2
"Phoebe, this is Juan."
"Juan, two, three, four, five, six, seven, eight."

Phoebe Seeing a Midget for the First Time, Age 2
"Mommy, did that man shrink?"

Pediatrician to Phoebe, Age 3
"Phoebe, what's your favorite vegetable?"
"Ring-Dings."

"Phoebe, what's your favorite fruit?"
"Ring-Dings."

Pediatrician to Phoebe, Age 3
"You're a very sweet little girl."
"Everyone seems to agree."

Mom to Phoebe, Age 3
"Where did Daddy take you for lunch?"
"Old McDonald's."

Grown-up to Phoebe on Telephone, Age 3
"May I please speak to one of your parents?"
"Do you want the Him or the Her?"

Me to Phoebe, the Yuppie Child, Age 4
"What would you like to drink?"
"Pepsier, please."

Phoebe to Her Dad, Age 5
"Daddy, what are you going to wear when you die?"

Me Explaining What a Report Card Is to Phoebe, Age 8
"Do you have any questions you want to ask Mommy?"
"Just one: Are they grading on the curve?"

Phoebe to Me, Age 10
"Mom, what does it mean to be 'gay'?"
"It means if you're a girl, you like girls better than

boys. And if you're a boy, you like other boys better than girls."

"Then I guess I'm gay, because I like girls much better than boys."

Phoebe to Me, Age 10, Seeing the Table of Contents for This Book
"Daddy has a chapter too?!"

2

What Do I Know? I'm Just Your Mother

TEACHING PHOEBE THE FACTS OF LIFE

Phoebe already knows the basics. She knows the world is round, the sea is salty, bears hibernate in winter, *Arkansas* is spelled like *Kansas* but pronounced totally differently. She knows the names of seven Indian tribes. She knows the Pledge of Allegiance. She knows that the barbican stands in front of the gatehouse in a medieval castle.

Now that she knows the essentials, I decided it was essential to teach her the immutable truisms and trivialities that will help her dress for success, read *People* magazine with greater perspicacity, shop intelligently at tag sales, and find the right shrink. I'm thinking of putting these on a laminated card so that Phoebe can carry it in her wallet for easy reference:

1. The chicken is done when the juice runs clear.
2. A lampshade's circumference should be the same as the height of the lamp's stem.
3. Meringue won't rise on humid days.
4. Always take on a 3–0 pitch.
5. The bidding ends when the auctioneer says, "Fair Warning."
6. Coats made with male mink pelts are preferable to coats made with female mink pelts.
7. You can't wear white shoes before Memorial Day or after Labor Day.

8. The word *tubular* is totally passé with surfers.

9. The color brown fades first on Oriental rugs.

10. Dogs do dream.

11. Cats purr only when there are people around.

12. It's bad luck to say "Macbeth." Instead say "The Scottish Play."

13. Never say "Congratulations" to a bride. Instead say "Best wishes!"

14. You can freeze milk.

15. It's harder to steal a base from a left-handed pitcher than a right-handed pitcher.

16. Never go to the hospital on July 1. That's the day the new residents and interns start.

17. It's tacky to carry a black pocketbook in the summer.

18. White chocolate isn't really chocolate.

19. Never call a "glove" a "mitt" unless you're a catcher.

20. All good shrinks go away in August.

21. Always step into the pitch.

22. *Servis est compris* in restaurants in France.

23. *List* means "retail" and *Net* means "wholesale."

24. Never wake a sleeping baby.

25. If you mix an SPF 2 suntan lotion with an SPF 8, you won't get an SPF 6.

26. Stay in the right-hand lane unless you're passing.

27. Never throw a cross court pass.

28. Tornados do hit trailer parks first.

29. The front mezzanine is the best place to sit for the ballet.

30. You can go from blond to brunette, but you can never successfully go from brunette to blond.

THE WELL-ROUNDED CHILD

Someone's going to make Phoebe read *Silas Marner,* *Beowulf,* and "The Week in Review" in *The New York Times* on Sundays. Let her hate *them,* not me. I want her to experience the pure joy of what's really culturally significant, from the early Rolling Stones to "I Love Lucy" reruns. I want her to know the Marx brothers and the Everly brothers as well as she knows *The Brothers Karamazov.* I don't ever want to hear her say, "Mom, who was Paul McCartney with before Wings? "I thought Armand Hammer was a baking soda," or "How come Senator Bradley has an N.B.A. ring?"

How can she possibly hope to lead a rich, full life if she doesn't know Cole Porter, George Gershwin, and Jerome Kern? Not to mention Elvis; Bill Haley; Peter, Paul, and Mary; Bob Dylan; the Kingston Trio; and the Grateful Dead? Who else is going to stress the importance of listening to Ella Fitzgerald singing Rogers and Hart, explain to her that everything ever sung by Louis Armstrong is sublime, let her know that there's no such thing as bad Nat King Cole, inferior Laurence Olivier, or mediocre William Faulkner?

Not to be harsh, but I believe that the child who doesn't know all the words to "When I'm Sixty-four," "Alice's

Restaurant," and "Get a Job" is a woefully uneducated child. The same goes for anyone who can't instantly recognize the music from *South Pacific*, hum the theme song from *M*A*S*H*, do a responsive reading at *The Rocky Horror Picture Show*. She can scrape by without knowing all of Stephen Sondheim, but she has to know some of it. *Parsifal* is important. *A Night at the Opera* is a must. Reading just enough of Virginia Woolf to say you've read it is good. Reading all the books about Virginia Woolf and the remarkable sexual proclivites of the Bloomsbury Group is even better.

Having standards in life is nice. Knowing standards is essential. So I'm diligent in making sure Phoebe knows everything from "I Can't Get Started," to "Blame It on My Youth," to "Autumn in New York," to "April in Paris." I'm working on teaching her Who's Who so that she never has to humiliate herself at a witty, urbane dinner party by asking "Who's that?" By the time she gets invited to dinner someplace other than McDonald's, she'll be able to converse intelligently about Marv Throneberry, Father Divine, Phil Spector, Pia Zadora, Pete Best, Jacques Cousteau, and Ted Bundy. And if, at the same dinner party, someone says, "To the moon, Alice!" "Rosebud," "Miss Clavell," "Fasten your seat belts, we're in for a bumpy ride," "I absolutely adore the Plaza!" "We'll always have Paris," "I don't know nuthin' about birthin' babies!" or "Yabba Dabba Do!" I expect my whiz kid, without missing a beat, to know the references.

I want her to know that "Everything's Coming Up Roses" doesn't count unless it's sung by Ethel Merman. That only George Rose can do justice to "I Am the Very Model of the Modern Major General." That she should never watch *High Society* when she can see *The Philadelphia Story*. That except for *Cabaret* and *Sound of Music* there aren't any movie musicals better than their Broadway originals. That everything Michael Bolton sings was already sung better by someone else.

Knowing when to laugh is important. So it's important that Phoebe be acquainted with W. C. Fields, Mark Twain, and Charlie Chaplin. I want her to know that Jerry Seinfeld is funny. Tom Hanks is funny. Roseanne Barr is funny. Tom Arnold isn't. Steve Martin is funny. Dean Martin isn't. Jerry Lewis is funny only in France, which is kind of funny.

Who else but her wonderful mother would teach her the movies not to go see: *Ryan's Daughter, Dr. Zhivago, Apocalypse Now, The World According to Garp, Love Story* (or anything else with Ali McGraw), *Rambo* (or any other epic with Sylvester Stallone), *Howard the Duck, Ishtar*, or any movie with Roman numerals after the title.

You can't be well educated or well rounded unless you understand human relations. And you can't understand human relations unless you've seen every movie Truffaut ever made, watched Katharine Hepburn act with Spencer Tracy, listened to Maria Callas, seen all the reruns from the "Mary Tyler Moore Show," cried at the end of *The Velveteen Rabbit* and *Charlotte's Web*, watched Fred Astaire and Ginger Rogers in *Swing Time*, heard what Aaron Neville, Frank Sinatra, or Charles Aznavour can do with a love song, read *The Magic Mountain* and Doris Lessing, danced to Artie Shaw's version of "Stardust."

Human relations tend to lead to Major Life Events. Major Life Events call for songs to celebrate them. So I've taught Phoebe "Havah Negilah" for bar mitzvahs, "The Bride Cuts the Cake" for weddings, "Ninety-nine Bottles of Beer on the Wall" for bus trips to camp, and "O Canada" for ice hockey games.

Speaking of songs and speaking of ice, let's talk about Christmas. I don't want even to think about the possibility of Phoebe someday trimming a Christmas tree listening to Alvin and the Chipmunks' holiday album or Tanya Tucker singing "I Saw Mommy Kissing Santa Claus." I prefer to think of her listening to Sir Thomas Beecham's *Messiah*, Benjamin Britten's *Ceremony of Carols*, and Phil Spector's Christmas album. While she wraps a great big present for me.

Of course the best present of all is turning out a child who can speak pig Latin as fluently as she speaks Latin, who knows when to skip the book and go directly to Cliffs Notes, who can thank her mother for this most liberal of liberal-arts educations by referencing a refrain from one of our seminal musical influences. All together now: "Mommy, Mommy, Bo Bommy, Banana Fana Fo Fommy, Fi Fie Foe Mommy, Mommy!"

EVERYBODY INTO THE GENE POOL

Long before I was a gifted wife and mother, I was a gifted scientific scholar. As far back as high school I had a keen interest in genetics and Mendel. And although it was only one semester in science class, I distinctly remember that Mendel was a monk who did something with sweet peas that made all the other monks and nuns understand genetics. I also know that planaria can regenerate, the Krebs cycle has something to do with citric acid, and that if everyone on the earth jumped up and down at the same time, nothing would happen.

Based on that dazzling scientific background, I think I have a better understanding of dominant and recessive genes than the average layman. I know that it's rare for two brown-eyed people to have a blue-eyed child. It's unlikely that a brown-eyed person and a blue-eyed person would have a blue-eyed child. And two blue-eyed parents will always have a child with blue eyes. The only scientific variables are tinted contact lenses and extramarital affairs, but let's not get into that.

So, in the simplest scientific terms, I've explained to Phoebe why she has blue eyes. I've also, in the completely unbiased way we scientists have, let her know that because of genetics she can thank her mother for her lovely, long coltish legs, her quick wit, her sunny disposition, her above-average intelligence, her glossy blond hair, and her improbably white teeth. I've even given her an example to prove it: When she and I go someplace and a total stranger takes one look at Phoebe, turns to me and bursts out, "Oh, my God, she looks exactly like you!" *That*, I tell Phoebe, is genetics in action.

"But," asks Phoebe, "what about Daddy?" Where does he figure in the family gene pool? Sad to say, but Daddy is somewhere down in the shallow end of the pool. Physically Phoebe has his earlobes and his dark eyelashes, which is no small thing. And of course he's 50 percent responsible for those gorgeous blue eyes. But I've pointed out to Phoebe that it's really in other areas that she shares genetic traits with her father.

From the man who has never in his life thrown anything out, on the theory that even an old ballpoint pen could come in handy someday, Phoebe has inherited the Pack Rat gene. And it must be very dominant, because in addition to old ballpoint pens, our house is also the repository for treasures such as one spike heel from a long-lost Canadian Barbie, yo-yos minus their string, and a miniature deck of playing cards with no aces.

Tom and Phoebe also share the "It's Too Hard to Put It in the Dishwasher, So I'll Just Leave It in the Sink" gene. Along with the "Why Pour the Milk into a Glass When You Can Drink It Straight Out of the Carton?" gene. And it's Tom's strong Procrastination gene that makes it impossible for Phoebe to leave for her seven twenty car-pool before seven nineteen, while she starts eating her breakfast at seven sixteen and begins looking for her school bookbag at seven eighteen, although she's been blaming me for the whole thing since seven fifteen.

I asked Phoebe if she remembered the time she was three years old and we told her she couldn't have another chocolate chocolate chip ice-cream cone and she had such an enormous temper tantrum that she threw up right there in Häagen-Dazs? *That,* I told her was early evidence that she had inherited a rare combination of two of her father's genes: the Instant Gratification gene and the Can't Tolerate Frustration gene.

It's uncanny how Phoebe and her father often ask me the same kind of question, such as: "Where's the milk?" The fact that I have to remind them both that in our house we keep the milk in the refrigerator just proves that they both suffer from the Short-Term Memory Loss gene. A man who would say, "Why make the bed? We're just going to sleep in it again in a few hours" has a strong Fallacious Reasoning gene. And not surprisingly he also has a daughter who truly believes that it doesn't make sense to wash her hair, because it just gets dirty again so fast.

When Phoebe complains that the roller coaster was too slow, the ski trail was too easy, the horse wouldn't gallop, and Mommy wouldn't let her bungee-jump, that's the Thrill-Seeking gene she's inherited from her thrill-seeking daddy. And when she asks incredulously, "We're flying

coach!?" that's what I call Tom's Deposed Prince gene being passed on to his Deposed Princess.

Genes, I've explained to Phoebe, are an important determinant in our looks, our personalities, our view of life. They're also the most powerful inheritance anyone can get. Unfortunately, in Phoebe's case, they're pretty much the only inheritance she's going to be getting. But I prefer to look at it this way: Anyone can pass on stocks and bonds, multimillion-dollar family businesses, or islands off the coast of Maine. But what Mommy and Daddy (well, mostly Mommy) have given their sweet pea is priceless.

THINGS AREN'T REALLY WHAT THEY SEEM

Once in a while people say what they mean. The other 85 percent of the time people say what they think you want to hear, or else they just throw caution to the wind and say whatever they have to to make you think something is a whole lot better than it really is.

These are called euphemisms. The people who use them most are called lawyers, doctors, politicians, real estate agents, used-car salesmen, and advertising executives, although this is an area where we tread lightly, since Mommy's brilliant career is on Madison Avenue.

So before Phoebe's old enough to buy a used Yugo, get an estimate for remodeling her kitchen, or consider a once-in-a-lifetime chance at waterfront acreage in Arizona, here are a few common euphemisms I think she should know:

1. "This apartment is adorable! It's so cozy and charming." (Small and cramped.)
2. "This house is a Handyman's Special!" (A wreck.)
3. "The owner is negotiable." (Desperate.)
4. "Conveniently located. Walk to train." (It's on Main Street, right behind the deli and next to the Laundromat.)
5. "Your blind date, Mark, is very sensitive and easygoing. He's playing in the big football game this Saturday!" (Mark is a wimp who plays glockenspiel in the marching band.)
6. "Your work shows real progress!" (At least you're not getting any worse.)
7. (To a director, actor, or playwright) "Wow! I've never seen a play like it." (What a bomb!)
8. "Perhaps the finest luxury car in America." (Then again, perhaps not.)
9. "The doctor will be right with you." (As soon as he gets off the phone with his broker.)
10. "The doctor had an emergency. I'm afraid we'll

have to reschedule." (There was a last-minute opening at his tennis club.)

11. "With this new supersonic drill, this won't hurt a bit." (Did you ever see *Marathon Man*?)

12. "It'll only take a minute." (An hour, the whole afternoon, whatever. Plus tests, plus the follow-up visits.)

13. "You can have complete confidence. I've done this procedure hundreds of times!" (I think I saw someone do it once in medical school.)

14. "The doctor prefers that you pay now, rather than sending you a bill." (Actually we insist. You think we trust you?)

15. "I had a great time too. Let's get together real soon." (How about the twelfth of Never?)

16. "I couldn't even *think* of asking you to baby-sit on New Year's Eve!" (Be here by nine o'clock.)

17. "I'm afraid the estimate I gave you is a little low." (Can you get a second mortgage?)

18. "Please fasten your seat belts. We're experiencing a little turbulence." (We're in the middle of two thunderstorms, and the left wing just got hit by lightning.)

19. "Thank you for sharing that with me." (If I want to know what you feel, which I don't, I'll ask.)

20. "It looks great, but I think you'd be more comfort-

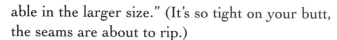

able in the larger size." (It's so tight on your butt, the seams are about to rip.)

21. "Seriously, don't do anything special for my birthday." (A little party, a cake, flowers, maybe a nice piece of jewelry.)

22. "Your son is so active! Have you thought about a children's sports program?" (Your son is a maniac. Have you thought about Ritalin?)

23. "Scientists claim this new wrinkle cream will work wonders." (They don't actually know, they just claim.)

3

~

My Other Child Is a Dog

BAD DOG, OLLIE!

My other child is a dog. A fluffy, happy, dopey, brown-and-white bearded collie. We named him Ollie, which we later realized rhymes with *folly*.

In spite of unconditional love, all the best schools, endless romps in the park, treats, trips, and his own blue plaid cedar-chip bed, Ollie is troubled.

Ollie is a compulsive and impulsive chewer. Triggered by some internal demon, he goes off periodically on what we refer to as search-and-destroy missions around the apartment, chewing to bits the object of desire *du jour.* Which could be anything from socks to sunglasses to cameras to the entire side of the sofa, when he's on a roll.

And his bite is worse than his bark. Forget "Drop it, Ollie!" — a command that means nothing when he's chewing a tasty pair of garden shears or a a juicy fountain pen. If you are so unwise as to try to take the offending object out of his mouth, he will simply bite part of your finger off. (In fairness to Ollie, Tom points out that Ollie doesn't really mean to bite, he just wants to hold on tight to whatever he's got in his mouth, and your hand is in his way. Oh.) My hand has been in the way three times, and I've got the tetanus shots to prove it. Another of Ollie's character flaws is his propensity to leap full-bodied, with a six-foot wingspan, on anyone he's particularly glad to see. And since Ollie, friendly to a fault, truly believes that a stranger is just a friend you haven't met yet, that's just about anybody. Here again, the "Ollie, off!" command means next to nothing.

So, being a New York kind of dysfunctional family, we got ourselves a top-notch personal trainer (one hundred dollars a house call). And Jody, the top-notch personal trainer, consulted her mentor, who suggested that we call in one of New York's top aggression therapists. Why do I know that none of this could happen in Iowa?

After a number of visits to our house to observe family dynamics and watch Ollie in his natural habitat, Jody was able to make a diagnosis. She explained that a dog thinks of his human family as a pack. And in observing the lopsided dynamics of our pack, it was obvious to her that Tom is the leader of the pack, Ollie is a close second in command, and I'm a very distant third. If Tom is the alpha dog, then I seem to be hovering slightly above omega. Phoebe doesn't count, since she and Ollie have evolved a healthy sibling relationship, which seems to consist of rolling around on the floor a lot and watching reruns of "Full House" together.

When Jody went into details about our problems, it got worse. She explained that since bearded collies are a working breed of dog whose ancestral job was to herd, Ollie's strong herding instinct had somehow emerged full-blown into herding his own little flock of one: me. I'm Tom's wife, I'm Phoebe's mother, I'm Ollie's sheep. I made the mistake of sharing this amusing revelation with my shrink, and three sessions later we're still exploring the implications of submission, low self-image, loss of control, and victimization in relationships.

Now that we've identified the problem (Baaa!), we're on an aggressive course of action to correct it. Jody says that within a matter of months we should start noticing some slight improvement. Her immediate advice was that I should start asserting myself as Ollie's master through rigorous behavioral modification. Since this would not yield immediate results, Jody suggested it might be wise to take some precautions.

She suggested that we warn everybody who was coming to our house that the minute we opened the door, they should scream "Off!" at the top of their lungs and at the exact same time lean over into Ollie's face to startle him as he leaps up. This maneuver required split-second timing and proved particularly ineffective with people such as the Chinese deliverymen, because of the language barrier and their understandable lack of interest in dog training.

Jody's other suggestion was that we put a sign on our front door that would read: HOLD ON TIGHT TO ALL YOUR VALUABLES. THE DOG IS GOING THROUGH A CRISIS. This made more sense to me than the "Off!" exercise, but it seemed so unwelcoming. I tried to imagine Jackie Onassis or Queen Elizabeth putting up a sign like that on her door and knew intuitively it wasn't something either of them would do. Since Ollie's life expectancy is fourteen years, I thought it just might make more sense not to have guests for the next eleven years. Plus, who wants to come over anyway clutching their gloves and pocketbooks, screaming at the dog, brushing mud and fur off their clothes during

dinner, watching him manically eat the wing chair out of the corner of their eye?

The other immediate course of action that Jody recommended was a little more extreme. We called it the American Gladiator approach. The drill was that whenever I saw that Ollie had something in his mouth, I was to race over to him, grab him by the top of his head with my left hand, grip the scruff of his neck with my right hand, make direct eye contact with him ("The eyes are the mirror of his soul," says Jody), scream "Bad dog, drop it!" in a Rambo tone of voice, hopefully catch him off guard, and then quickly flip him on his back until he dropped the offending object, at which point I would say sweetly, "Good boy, Ollie!"

If he wouldn't drop it, I was to tighten my grip, repeat my "Drop it, Ollie!" command in a louder voice, and drag him to another part of the room in an effort to get him into a more vulnerable, submissive position. The deal was I could never stop until I won, even if it took half an hour or the apartment was on fire.

Frankly these daily wrestling bouts were the most intensive exercise I've had since llama trekking or childbirth. Not to mention emotionally draining. Not to mention almost entirely fruitless. By the time I finally got Ollie to drop something after all that holding, tugging, pulling, screaming, dragging, wrestling, and flipping, I could retrieve the object only if it accidentally popped out of his mouth while he was trying to get a better grip.

Finally even Jody agreed that the Hulk Hogan therapy wasn't working. I had turned into a sheep that was a shadow of its former self. Ollie had turned into one confused shepherd. And worse, Jody could tell by looking into Ollie's eyes that instead of gaining respect for me, Ollie had lost his trust in me. So we immediately stopped the wrestling and worked on an interim regime of all-out kindness and compassion before we attacked the problem in a new way.

After only three weeks of my new Love Therapy, Jody announced that she once again saw Trust and Devotion when she looked into Ollie's eyes, and it was time to move on. Currently we're five months into our latest retraining, a Tough Love course designed to teach Ollie that I'm in control of him.

The rules are pretty simple. I'm the only member of the family who can feed him (he's supposed to learn that all good things come from me). I have to go through a five-minute series of basic commands with him every morning. And when I'm home, I have to make sure he is never out of my sight. He has to follow me, come when I call, lie down and stay next to me when I'm on the phone or watching TV. If he does wander off and return with something in his mouth, I'm supposed to look at him with Disapproval and Disappointment in my eyes and say sternly, "Bad dog, shame on you!"

When company comes over, I have to keep him on a

leash right next to me so that he won't jump or grab. The other night when our very brave neighbors came over for dinner, I actually made and served spaghetti with Bolognese sauce, garlic bread, and a salad while never once letting go of Ollie's leash.

I read somewhere that when people get dogs, their blood pressure goes way down because of the loving, companionable bond that forms. I know that my blood pressure has soared since we got Ollie. I'm always trying to remember what I'm supposed to be doing and saying to Ollie and remembering to say it in the right tone of voice at the right time and remembering to make direct eye contact with him, or it won't work. And finding recipes I can make and serve with one hand hasn't been easy either.

The good news is the rest of my pack has noticed some real, positive changes. I know all the commands, my eye contact is good, my attitude is improving, my attention span is longer, I'm working hard at my tasks, there's Commitment and Concern in my eyes. So while the jury is still out on Ollie, it looks like I'm making real progress. Good girl, Mommy!

OLLIE TAKES A BOW, WOW!

Ollie, a dog who has never seemed particularly stage-struck, recently became the latest member of my talented family to land a part at the Metropolitan Opera. Ollie, who is a bearded collie, played the part of a sheepdog in the third act of Verdi's *Falstaff* during the Met's 1992–93 season. Four arduous rehearsals, nine boffo performances, one national television taping! Talent? I'll say. Even Laurence Olivier didn't have to play another breed. Picture Rin Tin Tin with a three-octave range, picture Placido Domingo with fur! Star of the stage, pet of the Met! No wonder we call him Divo Doggie!

Animal magnetism and nepotism, a potent combination in anyone's life, propelled Ollie to the top. Ollie's raw talent, even temperament, stage presence, and breeding coupled with my husband's job as stage manager of the show helped Ollie win the coveted role. No other dog had a chance — and I mean that literally, since no other dog auditioned.

Not wanting Ollie to be nervous in front of four thousand people, and more to the point, not wanting him to leap into the orchestra pit (which I don't think our insurance policy covers), we signed Divo Doggie up for an intensive

acting class called "Your Pet in Show Biz," two months before opening night.

What a turnout! Ollie and Company, along with fourteen other multitalented dogs and cats with their aspiring owners, all hoping to get their big break. We discussed eight-by-ten-inch glossies, getting an agent, going on auditions, the heartbreak of rejection. All with the kind of camaraderie that hasn't been seen since *A Chorus Line* closed. Ollie and Phoebe (who would work together onstage for *Falstaff*) were chosen to be the demonstrators. They were asked by the teacher to do some simple obedience routines and walk-throughs, which actually turned into run-throughs since the floor was slippery and Ollie was pulling Phoebe in an effort to get closer to the terrified cats.

The highlight of the class was a surprise visit from

CNN, who wanted to tape the class for a special pet feature. One acting class, and already on national television! Unfortunately, as luck would have it, just as Phoebe was being interviewed, she and Ollie were completely upstaged by the late entrance of two masculine-looking women with a pair of miniature horses. All attention from then on was riveted on what I bitterly referred to as the Lesbians and Thespians. Phoebe was completely ignored, and poor Ollie sat dumbly through the rest of the class transfixed, trying to figure out what kind of dogs the miniature horses were.

After they recovered from their humiliating experience in acting class (did you see them on CNN, sitting behind the miniature horses?), Phoebe and Ollie spent the next two months rehearsing at home for opening night. Ollie was to enter stage left with Phoebe a few steps behind him dressed up as a Magic Fairy. He would walk all the way across the stage with her, lie down on cue, and stay quietly until the soprano finished her aria, at which point Phoebe would walk him offstage. Surrounding them onstage would be six principal singers, dozens of adult choristers, children, supers, the corps de ballet, one white horse, and one white sheep.

Rehearsals went well. Ollie worked like a you-know-what. Likewise Phoebe, the Magic Fairy, who carried a bag of doggie treats in her shoe to calm Ollie. Likewise Tom, who had to work hidden behind the stage curtain and keep his voice down when he called cues so that Ollie

wouldn't recognize him and come running. Early reviews were mixed, however, for Toots the horse, who was nervous and jumpy onstage. Equally unpredictable was Happy, the Bo Peep–looking sheep, who had a tendency to bleat when the singers hit a high note. Happy was actually fired at the dress rehearsal but got rehired on probation because everyone felt sorry for him.

The smell of the greasepaint, the roar of the crowd! Ollie loved it all — a day at the groomers, his own dressing room, a bowl of water every night from the stagehands, his new friends, Toots and Happy. And he got paid! A substantial check for each rehearsal and show. He actually got paid six times more than Phoebe — and try to explain *that* to your child. In an effort at achieving economic equity, Ollie and Phoebe traded salaries. Ollie's money went for grooming, taxis, and Milk-Bones. Phoebe's went for "Archie and Jughead" comics and college tuition.

How'd it go? Let's put it this way: Four thousand people let out a collective "Aaaah!" of surprise and delight when the Magic Fairy and the radiant white dog took their first enchanting steps onstage. Toots, alas, got replaced mid-run by Cody, a placid opera veteran who had successfully played the part of a horse in the previous season's *Fanciulla*. Happily, Happy stopped bleating and became a decorative part of the ensemble.

Of course the theater is full of unexpected drama. Happy and Ollie's budding friendship, unbeknownst to anyone, turned into a mad crush on Happy's part. Before

every performance Happy (a sheep) would follow Ollie (a dog) around backstage like a puppy, with Ollie acting shy and sheepish. Tragedy struck one Saturday matinee when Happy who could no longer contain himself, stopped munching his corn, got up stealthily, walked over and stepped on Ollie's head. Ollie, taken by surprise at this loving, albeit misguided gesture, stood up, let out a loud basso profundo bark and a couple of yelps as the audience laughed and Happy was forcibly removed from his inamorata.

Tragedy, comedy, melodrama, unrequited love, rave reviews — Ollie's fabulous opera career had it all. The show must go on, but it's going on without Ollie. Between stage fright (Phoebe's, not Ollie's), schlepping Ollie to the groomer at the crack of dawn, hailing taxis in the rain at night, hiding behind cardboard trees and bushes (Tom, not Ollie), we voted (three against one) to retire Ollie from show biz.

So now Divo Doggie is back playing the role he created and was meant to play — the role of the much-beloved, spoiled-rotten house pet, with a small but devoted fan club and a stack of fading eight-by-ten-inch glossies.

OUR DOG IS A EUPHEMISM

Our dog is so incurable that he thinks his name is "Ollie, Off!" Our dog is so dopey that he has trouble finding his water bowl, even though it's exactly where it's been for the past three years and seven days. Our dog is so dumb that his idea of how to play Frisbee is that we throw him the Frisbee, he catches it, then keeps it in his mouth all afternoon and won't let go.

Our dog is so talented that he won second prize in the Adult Novice category at the annual bearded collie picnic in Leonia, New Jersey, and we weren't the least bit surprised when many of our friends thought we'd said "A Dolt Novice." Our dog is so sweet that we sing the entire "Hallelujah Chorus" to him using his nickname, Ollie Collie, instead of the regular words.

Our dog is big and fluffy and licks your earlobe with his germ-ridden tongue when he is anxious. He is easily loved and easily misunderstood.

People Call Him:	*We Call Him:*
Manic	Playful
Wild	High-spirited
Crazy	Frisky

People Call Him:	We Call Him:
Stupid	Preoccupied
Aggressive	Driven
Untrained	Forgetful
Fat	Husky
Wimpy	Sensitive
Neurotic	Artistic

4

~

All in the Dysfunctional Family

ROMEO AND JULIET! LUCY AND RICKY! MOMMY AND DADDY!

"Tell me a story. Tell me a bedtime story," my little cherub asked. "Tell me all about you and Daddy." So this is the story I told her:

"Mommy, who in her salad days, was often mistaken for Grace Kelly, could have married anyone, from a prince to a filthy-rich Wall Street arbitrageur. But by the time Mommy decided to give up her carefree, bachelor existence, most princes had been deposed and all the filthy-rich arbitrageurs were in jail or halfway houses.

"So Mommy married Daddy. Daddy had been married once before, and you know what Samuel Johnson said about remarriage: 'A second marriage is the triumph of hope over experience.' So I hoped Daddy already knew how to buy an engagement ring, hire a band, and share a bathroom.

"It turned out Daddy could do all that and more! He could change a tire, fix a loose wire on a lamp, read a road map, sing the harmony on 'You Are My Sunshine,' lift heavy furniture, speak Italian, carry a canoe on his head, and buy so many remotes for the TV that you practically need a degree in engineering to watch '60 Minutes.'

"That's not all Daddy could do! He could make me laugh, keep me warm in bed at night, and answer the phone and tell my mother I'd just hopped into the shower and would call her back later. Daddy's very best quality was his unwavering conviction that I was smart, funny, and deserved to be taken care of.

"Of course, Daddy wasn't without his little quirks and peccadilloes. 'Too much ain't enough' was his philosophy in life in a few key areas: plants, computers, gardening gadgets, the aforementioned TV remotes, worldwide weather-monitoring devices, cable channels, cameras, fountain pens, pencils, antennas, CDs (not the money-making kind), tools, toiletries, ties, travel books, and telephones.

" 'Even a little is too much' was Daddy's philosophy when it came to any social occasion, especially one that involved my family.

"And even though Daddy went to college and graduate school in music (if you count graduate school at the University of Hawaii), imagine my surprise when I learned that Daddy couldn't make a bed, figure out how to get dirty clothes into the hamper, or screw on the top of the mayonnaise jar. Plus, Daddy, born in the U.S.A., also had a little trouble understanding the American currency system. When we first married, Daddy actually thought if you charged something, it meant you never had to pay for it.

"Once, Daddy was ordering designer socks from a department-store mail-order catalog and announced that he was getting fifteen pairs because they were such a bargain: only a dollar fifty a pair. Which would have been a real steal, except that it turned out the dollar fifty was the tax and shipping charge. The socks were about fifteen dollars a pair. Did we have a good laugh over that!

"Daddy's grammar is impeccable. Yet it took me six years to teach Daddy the difference between the verbs *need* and *want.* 'I need a new thousand-dollar laser jet printer for the computer,' Daddy would say. 'No,' I would say, 'You want a new laser jet printer.' 'We need a vacation in Rome this summer,' Daddy would say. 'No, we want a vacation in Rome.' *Need*, I would point out is: 'I need a new watch. Mine is broken.' *Want* is: 'I want a Rolex. I want a Range Rover. I want fifteen pairs of socks that I don't need.' " The fact that we spent so many years on this one lesson just goes to show how difficult the English language is. Not to mention how difficult Daddy can be.

"By the time you breezed into our life, Daddy and I had worked out some of the normal domestic snips and snaps that occur in any new marriage. We had learned to divide up the household chores equitably. I did everything; Daddy took the car in for its seven-thousand-five-hundred-mile checkup. We agreed to disagree. Daddy insisted that music played at a pleasantly low volume wasn't really music; I bought him headphones. I insisted I couldn't go to sleep with Daddy reading and the bed-table light on; Daddy bought me an eyeshade to block out the light, which didn't work, so now Daddy has to turn out the light when I'm ready to go to sleep whether he wants to or not.

"We realized that laughter is the best medicine: Daddy laughed so hard, I thought he was going into cardiac arrest the time my bathing suit came off at the Jungle Land Water Slide. I punished Daddy by making squid stew for dinner that night. We learned that some things would never change: I would always hate Daddy's ugly cactuses.

Daddy would always irrationally detest my enchanting collection of seashells that I have collected since I was ten. Daddy would always overcook my cheeseburgers on the grill. I would always make the chili too spicy, even though everyone else thought it was perfectly seasoned. We've learned not to hold grudges: In a few years I'm going to forgive Daddy for laughing at the water slide. Daddy almost never reminds me of the time I insisted I knew how to ski, then refused to get off the chair lift when it reached the top of the mountain because I was paralyzed with fear, even though what sadist would take a novice skier to a mountain only slightly smaller than Kilimanjaro and expect her to ski down sheer ice in near-blizzard conditions?

"But most of all and best of all and in spite of it all, we're still traveling along, singing a song, side by side. Happily ever after."

THEY'VE NEVER SAID, I'VE NEVER SAID

With the insight and wisdom imparted to me in middle age, I've observed that my life has fallen into a certain groove (all right, rut). Certain conversations, ques-

tions, situations, and responses are remarkably (all right, boringly) predictable. To wit:

My Husband Has Never Said:
   "Have you lost weight?"
   "We can't afford that!"
   "Maybe we should stop and ask for directions."
   "Let's get the taxes done early this year."

My Daughter Has Never Said:
   "How can I help?"
   "Of course I'll try one bite."
   "No, you go first."
   "Time to get up? Great!"
   "I'd rather have the piece of fruit."

My Mother Has Never Said:
   "You look so rested."
   "I'm so glad you married him."

My Therapist Has Never Said:
   "I don't think you need to come anymore."

My Dental Hygienist Has Never Said:
   "I can see you've been flossing every day!"

I've Never Said:
   "Gee, I'll have to have this taken in."
   "Emerald-cut diamonds . . . you shouldn't have!"
   "Give it to me [anything mechanical], I'll figure it out."

"It's my turn to walk him."
"You don't have to keep telling me you love me. I don't need constant reassurance."

The Mechanic Has Never Said:
  "It'll be ready a day early."

The Saleslady Has Never Said:
  "Your body is made for Spandex."

My Boss Has Never Said:
  "Not just a raise — a bonus!"

The Plumber/Painter/Electrician/Carpenter/Architect Has Never Said:
  "The estimate I gave you was way too high."

LOOKING FOR THE NINETIES

 I understood the eighties. It was so easy. Make a lot of money, spend a lot of money, go to David Hockney exhibits, order tiramisu for dessert, buy retail, know someone who knew someone who'd been on Malcolm Forbes's yacht.

It's the nineties I'm having trouble with. I know Yuppies are extinct and the "Me" Generation is now the "We"

Generation. I read the entire *Time* magazine cover story entitled "The Simple Life." I chuckled along with everyone else when Tom Wolfe dubbed this the Hangover Decade. I haven't said "If you've got it, flaunt it" for at least three years. I know Lacroix is Outré, fur is Passé, BMWs are Out, and outlets are In.

But I'm still confused. For example, *Time* says that mixed-breed dogs are In. For the life of me, I can't figure out how to break the news to our sweet, purebred bearded collie, Ollie. *Time* also says that the family is back. Well, I've had a family for the last thirteen years and they never left. Not even once.

Small towns are In, but they seem terribly expensive to me. The one Kim Basinger bought in Georgia cost her over three million dollars, and *People* magazine said the whole septic system has to be replaced. And how can this be the Hangover Decade if no one is drinking anymore?

When even vegetables are perplexing, you know you're in trouble. The latest Roper Report on trends that are going to shape the nineties states that "the creative use of green vegetables is going to be a key feature." Well, I could never cut my radishes to look like little roses, and now that my family's back, who's got time?

Then there's role models. I know enough not to buy the Franklin Mint Commemorative bust of Charles Keating, Tammy Faye Bakker, J. Edgar Hoover, or Woody Allen. But what about Michael Jordan? I want to be like Mike — he's a phenomenal basketball player, he gives to charities, he's on four out of five television commercials, he's every kid's role model, but he's betting millions of dollars on his weekend golf games? What about Jane Fonda? She went from making the world a better place with Tom Hayden to doing the Tomahawk Chop with Ted Turner. And I don't even want to talk about Beverly Hills breast implants.

I was very taken with a man named Peter Lynch, who just upped and quit his job to stay home and make peanut-butter-and-jelly sandwiches for his three daughters, until I got to the part that said he had built the largest stock mutual fund in the country and had a nest egg estimated at fifty million dollars. I think I'm sticking with Mother Teresa for another ten years.

But I guess I don't really need a role model to help me get back to basics and lead a simpler life. It's the nuances and subtleties that are really tripping me up. If baseball is simple, how come Roger Clemens is estimated to get $256,202 for every winning game? If the boardroom is Out and the backyard is In, can I finally put a heated lap pool in ours? Being poor is fine with me, but are you still allowed to have rich friends? Family reunions are very nineties, but is it wrong of me to want to have ours in Bermuda?

Even worse than figuring out the nuances of the nineties is this nagging fear I have: What if I get really good at *not* making money, we sell our house, give all the money to Sting to save the rain forest, move to Vermont, where my husband raises just enough hydroponic granola to pay Phoebe's 4-H Club dues and the nineties turn out to be an

aberration? That's why I'm holding on to my Mont Blanc pen, my Silver Palate raspberry vinegar, and the unlisted number of my masseuse who makes house calls.

GROWING PAINS

 My husband seemed pretty normal when I married him. Low-key, even-tempered, moderate. The kind of man who would say: "No more (FILL IN BLANK) for me, thanks. I've had enough (FILL IN BLANK) for one (FILL IN BLANK)." But that was before we got a house and I heard my husband utter the immortal words: "The house is great. But the yard could use a little work."

Have you ever noticed that every article you've ever read about gardening talks about how hard it is to be a gardener? I can't figure out why nobody talks about how hard it is to be a nongardener.

I'm married to a man I like to think of as my very own hardy perennial. Rain or shine, he's out on the South Forty by the crack of dawn weeding, feeding, seeding, staking, raking, propagating.

Oh, he isn't always gardening. In his idle hours he's out buying more plants, pricing mulch, or searching for the

perfect sprinkler head. He's off on day-long pilgrimages to distant nurseries. He's reading gardening magazines, gardening catalogs, or those incredibly expensive coffee-table gardening books that tell you how your backyard can look exactly like Sissinghurst.

I have nothing against gardens. I like them. But do a cutting garden, a rock garden, a kitchen garden, an herb garden, a rose garden, a vegetable garden, annuals, perennials, flowering shrubs, tropicals, heaths and heathers, citrus, and herbaceous borders on half an acre seem *de trop* to anyone but me?

I like flowers too. They look pretty. They smell good. I could see peonies and lilacs in spring, roses and daylilies in

summer, chrysanthemums in the fall, a Caribbean island in the winter. How about ninety-two kinds of flowers with names you can pronounce plus dozens of unsung heroes such as adonis, aconite, thalictrum, cimicifuga, euonymous, snakeshead fritillaria, veronica, and nicotiana? And that's just the tip of the iceberg, romaine, arugula, and mesclun at my house.

I have a theory: Moderation in everything. Try telling that to the man who owns five different kinds of garden shears and who pollinates his citrus trees by hand with a child's paintbrush.

Maybe I should have known when I married him twelve years ago and his sisters gave us a chain saw and a weed wacker for a wedding present. But despite our growing incompatibility, love continues to bloom, and I can honestly say our life is a bed of roses: New Dawn, Frau Dagmar Haustrop, Blanc Double la Coubert, Baroness Rothschild, Reine d'Holland, F. J. Grootendorst, and Rugosa.

MOM'S POP QUIZ

My family's always testing me — so why not? Some thought-provoking multiple-choice questions for everyone but Ollie, who has never provoked a thought in his life.

1. When we're finished with our half-eaten bowl of ice cream, do we:
    a. Leave it on the table because we know Slave Mommy will clean it up?
    b. Rinse it out and put it in the dishwasher?
    c. Put it on the floor for the dog to lick up?
2. When Slave Mommy tells us she's going on a business trip, do we:
    a. Mistakenly assume Slave Mommy will be drinking mai tais on the beach in Tahiti with bronze gods?
    b. Act sullen and moody until Slave Mommy leaves?
    c. Understand that Slave Mommy *has* to take business trips to boring cities with fat clients and eat in revolving restaurants if she wants to keep her job and support us in the style to which we've become accustomed?
3. When Slave Mommy comes home from a business trip,

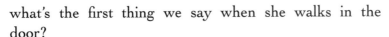

what's the first thing we say when she walks in the door?

    a. "What'd you bring me?"

    b. "You look awful"?

    c. "How was your trip? Let me help you with your bag. I missed you"?

4. When Slave Mommy cooks a special Near Eastern dinner from *The Silver Palate Cookbook*, do we:

    a. Say, "This tastes like kitty throw-up"?

    b. Say, "None for me"?

    c. Eat with gusto and compliment Mommy on her culinary zeal and sense of adventure?

5. When Slave Mommy is on the phone, do we:

    a. Interrupt her conversation by gesticulating wildly and screaming, "Where's my gym socks? I need them *now*"?

    b. Stand two inches away from Mommy, listening to every word she's saying and asking, "What did she say?" "Why is she canceling her trip?" "What kind of medicine does he want her to take?"

    c. Let Mommy talk as long as she wants and find something else to occupy us until she hangs up?

6. When Slave Mommy puts on her bathing suit for the first time all summer, do we:

    a. Make a face and say, "Sooooeeeee!"

    b. Point out that the varicose veins on her legs look even bigger this year than last?

    c. Tell Mommy that for one moment we actually thought it was Cindy Crawford coming out of the bedroom?

7. When Slave Mommy asks why *she* is always the one who has to make the bed, empty out the dishwasher, and put in the new roll of toilet paper, do we:

    a. Say smugly, "Because that's your job"?

    b. Look contrite and admit how thoughtless and insensitive we've been about the inequality of labor in the house?

    c. Say, "Shhh . . . I'm watching 'The Simpsons' "?

8. When we have a dirty Kleenex or a piece of gum we've finished chewing, do we say:

    a. "Here, Mommy"?

    b. "I've got a present for you"?

    c. "Excuse me while I put this in the trash"?

9. When Slave Mommy calls out, "Dinner's ready!" do we:

    a. Pretend we didn't hear her?

    b. Say, "Be right there!" and keep reading our book?

    c. Go immediately into the kitchen and say, "Gee, that smells good! Anything I can do to help?"

10. On Slave Mommy's birthday, do we:

    a. Remind her that if she had lived in colonial days, she would have been dead by now?

    b. Tell her that Lizzie's mother got a sheared-beaver coat and a Day of Beauty for *her* birthday?

    c. Sing "Happy Birthday," shower her with love and kisses, and tell her she's never looked younger, happier, thinner?

11. When someone calls and Slave Mommy is in the bathroom, do we:

    a. Say to the caller, "Mommy's going to the bathroom"?

    b. Keep banging on the bathroom door, shrieking, "Hurry up! Telephone!"

    c. Politely tell the caller Mommy's busy at the moment but will call back shortly?

12. If someone calls when Slave Mommy's not home, do we:

    a. Write down the name of the caller, take a message, and put it right next to the phone?

    b. Say, "I'll tell her you called," then forget all about it?

    c. Wait till Mommy asks, "Did Aunt Val call?" and then say, "Who? Oh, yeah. I think sometime last week. I'm sure I told you"?

13. If Slave Mommy can't remember how many feet are in a mile, do we:

    a. Say, "Anyone could forget that! Five thousand two hundred and eighty feet"?

    b. Yell, "Daddy! Mommy doesn't even know how many feet are in a mile!"

    c. Roll our eyes and give Mommy a look of disgust?

5

~

What I'll Never
Do to You
That My Mother
Did to Me

I GET ALL THE NEWS I NEED FROM THE WEATHER REPORT

Maybe it's just me, and I know I should feel good because the Year of the Woman was a big success, but I think it's harder than ever to be a wife and mother.

Just this morning I was walking past the newsstand and a headline popped out at me: WOMAN COMMITS SUICIDE — IN HER DISHWASHER. It was a standard front-loading machine that she'd pulled the racks out of so that she could fit herself inside it. They found her in the rinse cycle.

I can't imagine my mother killing herself in the dishwasher, although my mother was pretty tall, so I don't think she'd fit. And why would my mother ever have felt suicidal? She didn't work, we had a full-time maid (you were allowed to call them that when I was growing up). She had hats with flowers on them that matched her suits and she was president of our neighborhood civic association.

It was all so much easier in my mother's day. You didn't have to have a career. You didn't even have to have a job, except to be a candy striper or something. You could wear those bathing suits with little skirts, so you could eat like a pig and still go to the beach. You always voted Republican. You only needed one cookbook, *The Joy of Cooking*. You didn't have to figure out the difference between opaque, semiopaque, evening sheer, sheer satin, and evening-sheer control top.

There was no such thing as natural childbirth. My

mother had "twilight sleep," where they drug you into a swoon and then deliver the baby, whom you don't even know you've had until days later, when you wake up in your hospital room surrounded by flowers and a full-time nurse.

My mother certainly didn't have as much to worry about as we do. Happiness was a medium-rare prime rib, pots of coffee, sunbathing with baby oil, unfiltered Chesterfields, martinis, and french fries with gravy.

Back then you didn't have to worry about your kid divorcing you, paying alimony to your ex-husband, getting cancer from cellular phones, finding a therapist for your dog, getting your teeth bonded, having lead in your pipes or radon in your rumpus room.

Who's happy now? I mean really happy? Kathy Lee Gifford, who is so relentlessly, deliriously happy, I keep waiting for her to have a nervous breakdown right in front of Reege. Martha Stewart dressed in Armani, hacking away at Halloween pumpkins with her chain saw on the "Today" show, with Bryant Gumbel standing right behind her, looking dumbfounded. Brooke Astor is always smiling. No wonder. She's filthy rich, half of New York is named after her, and she's been widowed for years. Julia Child seems content: over eighty, married forever to someone taller than she is, and still eating all the foie gras she wants. Joyce Maynard seems to have found a sort of perverse happiness making a career out of writing about her divorce and her new kitchen with a jukebox.

As for me and every other domestic goddess I know, well, we're as happy as we can all be when we're not worrying about hiring illegal aliens, hoping the Scotch tape that's holding our hems up won't fall off during a client meeting, trying to remember what it is we're not supposed to eat to lower our cholesterol levels, and wondering what our kids are going to be telling their therapists fifteen years from now.

To be totally candid, even my mother wasn't 100 percent happy. I'll never forget the poignant childhood moment when someone asked my mother what was the single biggest change motherhood had made in her life and she thoughtfully replied, "I couldn't afford designer shoes." Good thing we didn't have a dishwasher.

THE BEGINNING OF MIDDLE-AGED REGRETS

Forget Edith Piaf—regrets are my life. Some big, some little. The good news is that I'm not a workaholic, a chocoholic, or a nymphomaniac. I guess the other good news is that I mostly love my husband and my daughter and my life and even my dog. But I'm not one to wallow in happiness.

One day on the bus home from work I started making a list of my regrets, and quite honestly I was glad I didn't live farther away.

Where to start? My family is so un-sports-focused that on the day of Super Bowl XXVII my husband didn't even know which teams were playing. Which led me to realize that for the rest of our lives we will be the kind of couple who never gets invited to a Super Bowl party.

In fact we're so out of it that one day when Phoebe was about five, I had a baseball game on TV and I overheard her exclaim, "Look, Daddy, he just hit the ball into the audience!" I had to explain to her that it's not like opera — it's called the stands. He hit the ball into the stands.

I'm not going to say too much about celebrity regrets except to share with you that Martha Stewart's new house in the Hamptons has eight bathrooms, all renovated.

One of my shallower regrets is that I am the only person in America who looks ridiculous in a baseball cap. Even Richard Simmons looks good in a baseball cap.

A profound but shallow regret is that I will never be able to wear any of the bathing suits in the *Sports Illustrated* swimsuit issue.

I regret that I know enough to know that no matter where we move to, we will always be living in what real estate people call a starter house. Whereas we would be living in Martha Stewart's house if I had only thought to invent Post-it notes, musical birthday cards, or Topsy Tails.

I regret I have a dearth of imagination. In ten years I have never given a theme birthday party for my daughter. Actually it never even occurred to me until recently. I was in the Party Store getting those imitation plastic Hawaiian leis for whoever won Charades at Phoebe's party and the woman behind me in line said, "Oh, you must be giving an Elvis party!" I didn't know right away what she was talking about. Two weeks later my friend Rosalie told me she was giving a troll-theme party for her son, which she hoped would be as successful as last year's dinosaur party, so I felt even worse.

I never R.S.V.P.'ed to my friend Wally's wedding, and that was fourteen years ago and now they're divorced.

I read the other day that Fife Symington is the governor of Arizona and I was shocked because I'd dated Fife Symington a couple of times in high school, and look where he is now. Certainly not in a starter house on the outskirts of Tucson pining for me.

I regret that out of all the languages I studied, pig Latin is my best. The other night Phoebe was learning a French song for school and asked me what it meant. After six years of French the best I could do was "Dance, dance, on your toes, with a sack of walnuts on your nose." If you had seen the look of utter disdain on her face.

When we go to Europe (not a hell of a lot, another regret), my husband (whose nickname is Larry Language) reminds me, "Whatever you do, don't open your mouth." When I studied Chinese in college, Mr. Chu, our professor,

immediately pegged me as least likely to succeed and would occasionally hand out homework assignments, saying, "This homework so easy, even Stephanie can do it." (Frankly, his English wasn't a lot better than my Mandarin.)

I regret that I am mechanically inept. Every time I rent a movie, I have to ask Phoebe to set up the TV and make it work for me. I regret, as does my entire family, that while I am an excellent driver, I have no sense of direction.

Two summers ago, driving home from the train station in Connecticut with Phoebe (which I have done hundreds of times), I got hopelessly lost and wound up in another state. (I only knew that because the man at the Citgo station told me.) Tom (not amused) had to come get us, with me standing out on a lonely median strip in the dark waving wildly and Phoebe inside the gas station crying, stuffing herself with candy bars and Yoo-Hoo.

Now I'm only allowed to drive where I've been before. In New York City I'm only allowed to drive from our apartment to the parking garage three blocks away. Sometimes, when I'm driving on the highway and see lots of cars in the rearview mirror, I think they're following me. So I go faster. That's the kind of thing I don't share with my husband.

Once in a while I am so overwhelmed at the enormity of my regrets that I do something mad and impetuous, like eat a whole pint of Chunky Monkey ice cream right out of the

container or go out and buy a pair of really expensive shoes that aren't on sale.

Which I then of course instantly regret.

ALL THAT'S STANDING BETWEEN MOMMY AND SAINTHOOD

There's no question that I could be sainted for the blind adoration I feel for my daughter, the depth of my devotion, the sacrifices I've made for her. But even saints have limits, not to mention neuroses. So while I'm the kind of mother who will pick the seeds out of watermelons for a child who should never experience even a moment of sadness or suffering, I'll never go with her inside a Portosan, speak to her coherently before I've had my coffee in the morning, or join her on any ride in the amusement park that makes a 360-degree revolution.

While I will painstakingly put Phoebe's hair into dozens of tiny braids to make it curly, even though the curls will only last a couple of hours, I will never pick up the daddy longlegs that's invaded her bedroom, watch "Beverly Hills 90210" with her, or show her my back somersault.

I will make my "fish" face and my "rat" face for Phoebe, but I'll never go camping with her, try to figure out her math homework, or bake her a birthday cake in the shape of a dinosaur, a bunny, or a mermaid.

I'll let Phoebe be the girl when we slow-dance, I'll even let her dip me. But I'll never take a fish off the hook for her, sew her a dress, or give her permission to marry a man who still wears his high school ring.

I'll buy dozens of boxes of Girl Scout cookies from my little scout, but I won't eat anything but the Thin Mints. I'll let her use my toothbrush, but I won't let her borrow my

lucky Cracker Jack ring. I'll buy her a dog or a cat or a goldfish, but I won't let her enter the science lottery at school, where the winner (who is actually the loser) gets the sowbug or the crayfish.

If we're out for a drive and gale force winds sweep the car into the ocean and we're sinking and the car is filling up with water and it's pitch-black and there's a man-eating shark trying to rip open the door and one of us has to sacrifice herself to the shark so that the other one can get out of the car and swim to safety, I would gladly die for my sweet child. But I could never let her watch me try on bathing suits or tell Daddy how much I really weigh, because that would kill me.

6

~

Now That I Have It All, Can I Return It and Get Credit?

SECOND OPINION

I don't care what they say about doctors charging outrageous fees for unnecessary operations and driving around in silver Range Rovers with cellular phones. I have great respect for the medical profession, even more so now that I see how unstinting they are in pursuit of new discoveries. You'd be gushing, too, if you'd been in the checkout line of the Stop & Shop last Tuesday, as I was, and saw a headline that took my breath away: THE DISEASE THAT MAKE IT IMPOSSIBLE TO LEARN MATH. The very disease that I have suffered with since I struggled to count from one to ten to graduate from nursery school!

I didn't have time to read the article because Tanya, my favorite checkout person, frowns on that kind of thing. And by the time I was back at the Stop & Shop the following week, I wasn't a bit surprised to see that the magazine had sold out.

What was upsetting to me was the fact that although I have had math disease since I was a little girl, no one even considered the possibility of this being a real, debilitating illness. Instead I heard cruel remarks from my parents and teachers, such as: "We'll explain it one more time," "You're just not trying," and "What do you mean, you don't get it?" If only I had had a doctor's note for Uncle Bill and Aunt Betty's Wee Care Nursery School explaining that I was too sick to get beyond nine.

Then I began wondering if there were any other diseases that these hardworking doctors, busy with their

tummy-tuck operations, their tennis games, and their junkets to Bermuda, just hadn't had time to get to. I mean it took Alexander Fleming years and years to discover penicillin, and he didn't even play golf. For all of us who have suffered with our afflictions in silence, never once complaining or malingering, I can only hope that these wise practitioners dedicate themselves to identifying even a few of the diseases that have kept many otherwise healthy people from leading rich, productive lives: the Disease That Makes It Impossible to Say No to Häagen-Dazs Triple Brownie Overload, the Disease That Makes It Impossible to Pass Up Sample Sales, the Disease That Makes It Impossible for Women to Find Bathing Suits That Fit.

Surely you, too, know someone who is chronically out of step at step aerobics, someone who still can't figure out if Michael Jackson and LaToya are the same person, someone with a lifelong inability to sleep on the other side of the bed. And what about the thousands who, try as they might, cannot stomach sweetbreads, college graduates who can operate computer modems but can't open a folding umbrella in the rain, Mensa members who face every day not knowing whether or not they locked the front door? And shouldn't there be even a small telethon for all those who can't get an even tan, who have never made good salad dressing, who listen carefully but can't understand a word the French waiter is saying?

Oh, it's probably too late for me and the millions of other math failures who never got beyond long division,

who scored lower than the school quarterback on our math SATs, who never offer to figure out who owes what in a restaurant for fear of humiliating ourselves. But for others who know the heartbreak of broken Totes, the shame of apologizing for oily vinaigrettes, the stigma of ordering in a restaurant in Paris, who have been led to believe that they are the problem, I hope that we can someday cure the disease and the ignorance that surrounds it. And I would like to add (I'd also like to multiply and divide), that I hope Aunt Betty and Uncle Bill rot in hell with a broken folding umbrella and a heaping platter of sweetbreads.

DEAR MARTHA

Dear Martha,

It's beginning to look a lot like you-know-what and I can't tell you how inspirational your book, *Martha Stewart's Christmas*, has already been. You've got so many nifty ideas for holiday entertaining and gift-giving, I don't know where to start.

I was going to make the three hundred English plum puddings, the way you always do — it sounded pretty easy, but I haven't been collecting English pudding bowls

like you have, so right away I was stumped. Then my boss wouldn't give me the week off when I told him I needed the time for baking plum puddings, so scratch that one.

And forget the lovely aromatic garden potpourris. I looked in my cupboard and found we were fresh out of hibiscus, allspice berries, bayberry bark, eucalyptus leaves, poppyseed pods, whole star anise, blue malva, lavender, rosehips, dried orange and lemon peel, Tellicherry peppercorns, orrisroot powder, and senna pods. (You should have seen the look on the clerk's face at the Stop & Shop when I asked her what aisle the senna pods were in!)

I know *you* like to get your friends and family together to whip up your favorite homemade relishes, conserves, condiments, jams, jellies, curds, vinegars, pomanders, cakes, cookies, stollen, puddings, fruitcakes, and wreaths, but when I suggested the idea to my best friend, Barbara, as a fun after-work activity, she said, "What, are you crazy?!" and hung up on me. I guess you have better friends than I do.

And you should have heard my family laugh, Martha, when I broached the subject of making our very own gingerbread mansion. I showed them the picture of yours — a five-foot replica of your picture-perfect Turkey Hill Federal farmhouse with the intricate gold-leaf roof, the battery-operated lights inside, the little topiary trees and gilded pinecones outside. What a great family project!

I was just enchanted with your homemade gift baskets, each with a different theme. Especially your Friendship Basket, a handmade ash picnic basket filled with a Christmas pudding, tea-smoked chicken, curried spiced nuts, cayenne-pepper wafers, Scotch-shortbread scallops, chamomile tea, mulled-wine mix, an old edition of Emerson's essays on nature, and pretty floral napkins. But with lazy friends like Barbara, even the cayenne-pepper wafers seem *de trop*, don't you agree, Martha?

Oh, and your annual Chirstmas party sounded divine! I loved the idea of 175 of your closest friends coming over for what you call "Christmas Around the House." Hors d'oeuvres in the outside kitchen; a lavish buffet supper in the barn; champagne, egg nog, and desserts in the main house; the choral group you bring in to sing carols. I envisioned a somewhat smaller version called "Christmas Around the Apartment," but Scrooge (that's what we call my husband at Christmas) said he's busy that night — and I didn't even tell him what night.

Entre nous, Martha, things aren't going quite as I had hoped. Maybe if I didn't have a full-time job, a husband who works like a dog, a dog whose obedience-school teacher insisted we get a tutor, and a ten-year-old who's already in sugar shock, I could have the Martha Stewart Christmas I envisioned. Maybe if I don't sleep

from now until December 25th, I could get to the homemade gilded wrapping paper, the cockscomb topiary, the cassoulet for one hundred, the copper cookie tree, the Hopi corn jam, the boxwood topiary, and the three dozen Nöel Nut Balls. Maybe the clerk will find the senna pods. Or maybe, Martha (and I know it's a lot to ask), you'll just invite us up to Turkey Hill for the big day. We do happen to be free, (I'll find someplace else for my mother-in-law to go), my daughter is just mad for Nöel Nut Balls, and I'm sure that the dog will be housebroken by then!

Hoping to hear from you,

SIX RMS. RIV. VU.

I recently read that the odds of winning the New York State Lottery are exactly the same as the odds of having all the air in your living room sucked out in the next five minutes. This must be about the same odds as getting a large prewar apartment in New York without paying thousands of dollars in key money, sleeping with your super, or offering the landlord your firstborn son.

While I am still waiting for the air to get sucked out of

the living room, I am happy to report that I just got a bigger living room for it to be sucked out of. I just got the *perfect* apartment. Three big bedrooms! River view! Eat-in kitchen! Parquet floors! Fancy molding! Walk-in closets! Top floor! Four exposures (possibly more, since there's currently a major leak in the ceiling). Dirt cheap!

I know what you're thinking: How nice for you. And I know what you're *really* thinking: Some nerve! How can *I* do it? In my case it was really quite simple: not big bucks, but six long years of charm, chutzpah, patience, warmth, wit, kindness, perseverance, and more chutzpah. If you don't mind taking an extended sabbatical from *your* life, you could be a real estate winner too.

It started a dozen years ago when I was living by myself in a small two-bedroom apartment. Somewhere along the way I gained one husband, one child, one housekeeper, one cat, and one dog. (The attrition rate has been surprisingly low — the only one I've managed to lose so far is the cat.) When I could no longer turn a corner without tripping on a roller skate, a banana-seat bike, or a barbell, I called up my landlord. "I need a bigger apartment," I said. Mr. Sagarin laughed. "So does everyone else in New York," he said pleasantly as he quickly hung up the telephone.

An inauspicious start. I changed tactics. I found out from my super than my landlord was a big opera lover. *Mirabile dictu!* My husband works for the opera. I called my landlord back. "I just happen to have two tickets [so they cost me $150] for *La Bohème* with Pavarotti and Freni and

wondered whether you'd like them." "How thoughtful of you, Miss Pierson," he replied, remembering my name for the very first time.

Luckily Luciano was in good voice. The tickets were followed (at the proper intervals) with handsome wreaths, homemade pomanders, exotic potpourri, homegrown tomatoes, out-of-season tulips, home-baked cookies, Get Well cards, Stay Well cards, Valentine cards, Hanukkah cards, and Christmas cards. (I think I sank to my lowest with the card featuring a picture of Phoebe as a baby, sitting with the cat, both of whom I had artfully propped on a sled in front of the building.)

Then two wonderful things happened. Through thank-you notes and telephone pleasantries I developed a real affection for Mr. Sagarin. And I scored a major hit with a song I wrote for him one Christmas. My husband's colleague recorded it for me. It's sung to the tune of *Rigoletto's* "La Donna è Mobile." I'm including the lyrics in case your landlord's name rhymes with "Sagarin."

> We love our little place,
> But we've run out of space.
> Our hearts are gloomy . . .
> Our rooms aren't roomy.
> What a sweet little place,
> All that it lacks is space.
> We've looked but cannot find,
> The dream we have in mind.

Molto desperation! *Piccolo* location!
Grandissimo frustration!
It's just too small!
Too small . . . Too small . . . *Troppo* too small!
Too small . . . Too small . . . *Troppo* too small!

So, Mr. Sagarin,
Pity the fix we're in!
Think of us when a three
Bedroom apartment's free.
Oh, Mr. Sagarin!
Here come the moving men!
We will leave *subito,*
Just tell us where to go!
How can we make it clearer? We'll spend lots of lira,
Are we any nearer
Our nice new home?
New home, new home, our nice new home!
New home, new home, our nice new home!

Cute, said my husband. Shameless, said my friends. Obsessive, said my shrink. Weeks turned to years. Even I was beginning to despair. I ran out of lyrics, I got tired of baking sugar cookies in the shape of tiny penthouses. My daughter told me that she absolutely wouldn't pose for one more Christmas card.

And then one day I got the Call. "Miss Pierson?" "Yes, Mr. Sagarin." Pause. "We just happened to get a three-

bedroom on the river. Would you be interested?" Two minutes later I was breaking out the Moët & Chandon. It's amazing how cold champagne gets after it's been on ice for a couple of years.

─◦─◦◦─◦─

I BRAKE FOR CENTER-HALL COLONIALS

I used to be passionate about passion. Then I got married. After that, I was passionate about Julia Child's Boeuf Bourguignon, antique pillow shams, and amusing white burgundies.

Then I had a baby and a puppy. After that I was passionate about teething, hugging, Scotchguarding, and saying no in a loud, firm voice.

Now my daughter's in fifth grade, my dog has finally figured out where the front door is, and my husband is grateful for microwaved chicken pot pie.

Nature abhors a vacuum. I have a new passion: house hunting. Not just any house: a country house. Not just any country house. Certainly not the small, unassuming weekend house we have now. We're talking center-hall

colonials, side-hall colonials, eyebrow colonials, Greek Revivals, ex–country inns, stone farmhouses, pre-Revolutionary farmhouses, carriage houses, antique schoolhouses, 1790 Capes, country estates.

Real estate listings are my life. Real estate brokers are my closest friends. I say, "Hi, Marcia, got anything in Katonah?" the way kids play Go Fish and say, "Got an ace?"

As with all grand passions, it's the small things that drive me wild: "thirty bucolic acres," "six-stall barn," "heated pool," "swimmable pond," "gazebo," "wainscotting," "renovated kitchen," "double porch," "five fireplaces," "wideboard floors," "two staircases," "outbuildings," "part of estate," "stone walls," "mature plantings," "flagstone terrace," "beehive oven," "french doors," and my personal favorite somewhere deep in Bucks County: "stone milkhouse." I don't even know what it is, but I can't live without it.

Of course I know what *not* to look for too. Listings that boast: "aboveground pool," "sliders to deck," "new aluminum siding," "friendly neighbors," "lots of kids," "minutes from interstate," "walk to town."

Being the introspective person I am, I often ask myself if I'm asking for too much. I don't think so. Only for a house so filled with vintage charm, so reasonably priced, so spacious, so gracious, so totally, quintessentially perfect that it will guarantee that my life will be perfect too.

Fantasy 1: I'm standing in the renovated kitchen of my

farmhouse canning peaches from our own trees. Sunlight is pouring through the original leaded-glass windows. I'm wearing a simple homespun gingham dress from the Ralph Lauren Country Collection and those cute gardening clogs from Smith & Hawken. My husband is outside pruning the wisteria and watering the hollyhocks. I hear my daughter's merry laughter as she canters across the meadow in her antique ponycart. The dog finds the front door the day we moved in.

Fantasy 2: It's always sunny, there's no mud in March, the pipes never freeze, my husband's Big Boy tomato plants produce at least one ripe tomato before the deer eat them, my daughter isn't allergic to goldenrod, I never step on a slug in my bare feet, my mother-in-law loses our phone number.

You say, "motivated seller," "relocation," or "carrying two mortgages" and I'm a motivated looker. I can walk into a house and figure out within ten minutes whether my pine armoire will fit in the guest bedroom, what color to sponge the dining-room walls, and whether I'll be able to hear my daughter playing her drums in the attic while I'm standing in the pantry.

You know how there are certain things you can't tell your shrink because you just know you'll spend *weeks* in therapy talking about it and your shrink will manage to take the wind out of your sails the minute you try to explain the whole thing calmly and rationally? This is right up

there with not ever revealing the recurring dreams I have about my butcher, who is sixty years old and has hair growing out of his ears.

My shrink sometimes asks, "Are you still looking at houses?" and I hear myself saying, "Oh, once in a while." Do you think I'm going to pay good money to hear hostile Freudian questions like "Are you looking for a house or a fantasy?" "Do you realize that the more accessible a house becomes, the less desirable you seem to find it?" and "Let's talk about your fixation with wraparound porches."

I say let's talk about the only true passion I've ever known where I get to fall in love constantly, never have to take off my clothes, and save approximately $300,000 every weekend.

HONEY, I SHRUNK THE HOUSE

So I'm reading *The Wall Street Journal* the other day, and right smack next to an article entitled U.S. RESERVES OF OIL TOP PAST ESTIMATES is an even more exciting headline: HATE YOUR HOUSE? CLARE MARCUS MAY BE COUNSELOR YOU NEED.

Far out. A shrink for your house! Guess where Pro-

fessor Marcus lives? That's right. She teaches psychology at the University of California at Berkeley and she believes that through her unique Jungian-inspired therapy you can find out if you and your house are compatible.

She has her clients talk openly to their house, expressing any problems or concerns. Then they pretend to be

their house and answer back. "Clients are nearly always far more honest and insightful when they allow themselves to speak as their house," Professor Marcus says. "As the house they can get quite emotional."

Really far out. Professor Marcus charges one hundred dollars for these revelatory role-playing sessions and gives a number of inspiring examples of homeowners who sorted

out all kinds of ambivalence, love-hate conflicts, and latent maternal grudges through counseling.

Being a big believer in self-therapy and having skimmed *The Road Less Traveled*, I felt eminently qualified to skip the hundred-dollar session and role-play my feelings directly with my own house, a simple 1930s bungalow in Connecticut. I was astonished at the results and would like to share the transcripts with you.

TRANSCRIPT

ME: Hello, house.

HOUSE: How are you?

ME: I'm fine. Well, not so fine. We have to talk.

HOUSE: What's up?

ME: Things aren't going as well as they could. My feelings for you have, how to put this delicately, diminished.

HOUSE: What do you mean?

ME: Well, I used to love to walk in the front door. You were so warm and welcoming. Everything was fresh and new.

HOUSE: So?

ME: Now all I see are your flaws. You run out of hot water when I'm taking a shower. The basement floods when it rains. And no matter how hard we try, we can't get those scratches off the living-room floor.

HOUSE: (*whispers*) You've got crow's feet and you're putting on weight.

ME: What?

HOUSE: Nothing.

ME: The other thing is, you used to seem so spacious. Now you feel cramped and small. Almost claustrophobic.

HOUSE: Maybe you should get rid of that enormous ugly sofa you paid too much for. And that big lug who always tracks mud all over the place. You could live without him.

ME: That's my husband.

HOUSE: You married a man who still can't build a fire without the whole room filling up with smoke? What about the hyperactive one who Rollerblades all over the house with the Walkman stuck in her ears?

ME: That's my daughter.

HOUSE: I'm sorry. How's the dog doing with his aggression therapy? I couldn't believe he chewed through all the legs on the dining-room table.

ME: He's just going through a phase. He's acting out.

HOUSE: And you're worried about not getting enough hot water?

ME: You're extremely confrontational.

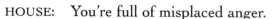

HOUSE: You're full of misplaced anger.

ME: Your problem is a personality disorder and a latent pathological rage.

HOUSE: Which isn't half as bad as being a chronic malcontent with the most dysfunctional family since the Mansons.

ME: *This* is coming from a sadistic Money Pit, whose only joy derives from inflicting pain on a defenseless family of innocents?

HOUSE: And you have mice.

ME: A cruel, deep-seated need to hurt and humiliate —

HOUSE: Not mice. You have rats. As big as Willard. Bigger.

ME: (*calling out*) Oh, who's that at the door? Excuse me. Why, it's the nice lady from Century Twenty-one. Come right in!

HOUSE: Rabid rats. Packs of hungry, rabid rats.

COMPROMISING POSITIONS

Every family has its secrets. The only difference is that I am indiscreet enough to share ours. My hus-

band's second cousin got indicted for insider trading. My great-uncle left my great-aunt for a nineteen-year-old topless dancer with cellulite. My brother-in-law and his wife belong to a California religious cult that beams them up to Uranus. Guess what? Now we've got an even worse secret: I just bought a La-Z-Boy.

Yes, the Rube Goldberg of American mechanized comfort. The chair that screams out "Dad!" "Den!" and "Dayton!" And we don't even belong to a bowling league.

Actually it all started with a recurring dream I used to have. In it the doorbell rings and it's Mario Buatta coming to visit me. (Once it was Andrée Putman, but that was the night I had a double espresso and two brandies at dinner.) Mario comes in, takes one look at my house, and says he had never seen anyone with a talent for decorating like mine.

He gushes over my cabbage-rose chintz and my tiny, tufted Victorian slipper chair. He is mad for my crystal obelisks and my majolica collection. He says he'd kill for the portrait of cavorting Jack Russell terriers over my fireplace. Then he asks if he can use my phone so that he can have Mark Hampton and Ralph Lauren rush right over. Wow!

I would have asked my shrink what it all meant, but I know from experience that decorating dreams take at least three grueling sessions and you never really get to the bottom of them. Plus I haven't had that dream for months.

It ended about the same time *The New York Times* said crystal obelisks were passé and my husband said he was never going to stay up and watch the Academy Awards with me again unless we got a comfortable chair. A really comfortable chair. A chair as comfortable as a You-Know-What.

Which is all directly related to how I got to wandering around the furniture department of Macy's and seeing a vision: a recliner like no other. A delicate, sculptured wing chair covered in white linen (yes, a natural fabric!) with graceful wooden legs. And when I sat in it, its little attached ottoman sprang out silently to support my feet. I leaned back in bliss, and the next thing I knew I was saying, "When can you deliver it?"

So the Family Secret is now in my living room, out in full view. I told my husband I got it just for him. (Of course he still falls asleep before the talent part of the Academy Awards.) And to get even more mileage out of it, I told Phoebe and Ollie the same thing. It looks great, it's obscenely comfortable, and everyone fights to sit in it.

I did have a few second thoughts about buying it. Now that I owned a La-Z-Boy, would I start getting cravings for Cheez Whiz and those potato chips in the tennis-ball containers? Would I want to start collecting Hummel figurines? Would I buy sundresses to match my daughter's? So far there's no sign whatsoever that it's catching.

I love my La-Z-Boy. I don't even care that the very

name is both illiterate and sexist. And I'm glad I'm not having my recurring decorating dream anymore. I mean, can you imagine trying to explain to Mario or Andrée what I'm doing with a contemporary colonial-faux wing chair that turns into a fifties Midwest recliner with a movable ottoman?

—❧—✿—☙—

ME AND MARTHA STEWART— OUR BUSY YEAR

I always think I'm doing great. Then I see what Martha's up to. I recently compared one whole year of my life with a year of Martha's via her magazine, *Martha Stewart Living*. If Martha's spectacularly overachieving year sounds like I exaggerated or embellished in any way, believe me, I didn't. I wish I were that creative.

January

Martha wrote thank-you letters for Christmas gifts and hospitality, recycled the tree, started herb seedlings in the greenhouse, forced more narcissus (more narcissus than

what?), rooted houseplant cuttings for container plantings, whipped up an amusing potato-with-arugula-and-curly-endive soup, baked red-cabbage-and-onion tarts, and candied hundreds of innocent kumquats.

My January highlights included gaining five pounds from Christmas, paying bills for stuff we already broke, and researching liposuction. I didn't have to write a lot of thank-you letters for gifts and hospitality, if you know what I mean.

I also baked a double batch of Pecan Squares the night before Phoebe's birthday party at school. Unfortunately our chain saw was in the country, so I couldn't cut them. When I did manage to pry one out of the pan, it had the taste and texture of baked cement, so I had to race to the deli at eleven P.M. to buy thirty slices of pound cake, which I rewrapped and put in my own baking tins.

February

A big month for Martha and me! Martha met someone who was able to explain chocolate to her. So she whipped up thirty-three pounds of chocolate leaves, flowers, fruits, swags, and cabbages.

Then she met someone who taught her how to make needlepoint pillows.

Then she already knew someone who taught her how to make Brazilian food. Martha didn't make swags or cabbages, the way you might expect. But she did make a

fifteen-pound roast suckling pig on a banana leaf, toasted farinha, moqueca, and yuca. (I'll say.)

In between that (does this woman sleep?) she whipped up a two-tier flourless chocolate cake filled and frosted with ganache and decorated with handmade chocolate leaves, crafted a Raspberry Ruffle, and lovingly prepared a romantic Valentine dinner.

As for me, I did a little creative writing (re-creating lost receipts and diaries for our exciting upcoming tax audit), discovered a divine new Chinese restaurant to order from, made a romantic Valentine dinner à trois for me, Phoebe, and Ollie, since Tom was working that night, then pulled my back out lifting Phoebe's bed looking for a lost Game Boy game. I didn't meet anyone who introduced me to chocolate, needlepoint, or suckling pig.

March

In like a lion, out like a lamb! Actually in Martha's case In like a lion, out like a lion! Martha learned all about American architecture, majolica, and beans. She also figured out how to make drop-dead serving trays from an old tray, a piece of glass, and some well-chosen odds and ends. Frankly, trays that took her less than an hour to make looked better than any wedding present I ever got, which would have depressed me if I wasn't so proud of Martha.

Martha also found time to get black spots off her roses

with sulfur-based fungicide, degradable fatty-acid soap, and petroleum-based dormant oil spray.

Not to brag, but I was no slouch either. I hemmed one of Phoebe's school uniforms in under two hours, cleaned the fish tank, threw out all the stuff in the refrigerator that had mold in it, worked overtime in the office two weekends and at least five nights, and had Ollie's half brother, Dylan, over for a playdate, which they both enjoyed very much.

I learned all about root canals, cabin fever, and why happily married women run off with their aerobics instructors.

April

Easter! Not a cloud in the proverbial sky! Martha did herself proud with everything from the maple-glazed baked ham to a handmade eggshell vase filled with pansies, and hens' eggs brushed with egg white and covered with gold leaf.

Easter! I ordered one of those honey-baked hams, pre-cut in spiral slices, since Tom has all the meat-cutting finesse of Freddy Krueger (believe me, you'd never know his father was a surgeon). My in-laws came for dinner and brought that sweet-potato casserole we all love with the canned pineapple chunks and artificial marshmallow bits. My brother and sister-in-law baked their own bread (I don't know how they got the Wonder Bread recipe).

Ollie somehow got into Phoebe's Easter basket, ate five of her Cadbury peanut butter chocolate eggs still in the plastic wrapper, and had a diarrhea attack in the living room. We hid fifteen eggs throughout the apartment for Phoebe and her cousins. Somehow we only found fourteen, but Ollie, hunter extraordinaire, found the last one two weeks later.

May

What's the first thing you would do if you'd just finished restoring a weekend house? Relax? Pour yourself a stiff Scotch? Don't be ridiculous! You'd be painstakingly painting all the beaded-board ceilings throughout your house in unusual shades to match the vintage paint chart of early twentieth-century flower colors you'd unearthed at an antiques fair. P.S.: Martha's butler's pantry now has a mauve ceiling, the color of creeping-thyme flowers.

While Martha was mixing the Larkspur Pink and Aurelian Lily Orange, I was meeting with the IRS auditor, working like a dog, walking the dog, renewing my driver's license, and helping out at Phoebe's school book fair. And my social life was positively Ivanaesque: We joined the Potato of the Month Club, I had dinner at a restaurant with my friends Robin and Carol and didn't get home until nine-thirty, our neighbors came over and I ordered pizza, and my mother-in-law stopped over to borrow our opera glasses.

June

Martha was gilding mirrors, making a succulent wreath (all you need is two hundred succulent cuttings and a patented wreath frame), and cleaning rugs. Did you know that the best soap for cleaning rugs is also the best soap for cleaning racehorses? Martha didn't make a joke about one soap cleaning all your runners, but I don't know how she'd have time for levity, considering all she does.

Such as orchestrate a fabulous charity party at her beach house for 717 people. The party (surprise!) was a huge success.

Sometimes I feel like we were separated at birth. I gave a party too! A barbecue in the country for Tom's colleagues at work and their families. The bugs were so bad (I don't know why they call them no-see-ums, when you can see them perfectly well) that Tom had to grill the turkey dogs wearing the hat with the mosquito-netting veil while the rest of us stayed inside. Ollie got so excited at having company that he ate two citronella candles and drank someone's gin and tonic.

July

If there is one thing in life that defines the essential difference between Martha and me, it's this: a handmade picnic hamper. Martha started hers with a five-dollar thrift-shop suitcase; she ripped out the old lining, relined

the inside after she'd strengthened the fabric with fusible interfacing, then she secured the harness, cut some book-board, hemmed, hammered, mitered, hinged, and hot-glued her way to success. Way to go, Martha!

We had picnics and outings too. We visited my mother's best friend at a fabulous alcohol rehab center in Pennsylvania that you would have sworn was some fancy spa if you didn't know better. My mother-in-law stayed with us Fourth of July weekend in the country and never got out of her nightgown except to go to the town Fourth of July parade. Phoebe and her friend, Sasha, had a lemonade stand at the parade and made $6.20, which they spent on Jolly Ranchers and Gummy Worms to rot their teeth.

August

The lazy, crazy, hazy days of summer! Lazy? Martha? She restored wicker chairs, researched old-fashioned roses, and created a blue drink in her blender that looked frighteningly like Windex. After that Martha did an extensive study of stain removal — everything from motor oil to lipstick to red wine. (I have a feeling that if you spilled that blue drink of Martha's on your clothes, you might as well just forget about it.)

Martha explained the best way to cope with a worst-case scenario: red wine, vinegar, and Tabasco sauce spilled

onto a linen handkerchief (I can identify with this). All
you have to do is sprinkle cornstarch on to soak up the
liquid, blot, scrape off the stain with a credit card, bleach
the spill area with a solution of water and white vinegar
applied with an eye dropper, then spread the fabric over a
bowl and pour boiling water, from a height of about one
foot, directly onto the discoloration and gently pat the
fabric to encourage absorption. Or you could just throw
out the handkerchief and get to work on Martha's next
project, embroidering dots (sixty-one dots) on homemade
napkins.

After six lazy, crazy, hazy summers Tom finally put up a
hammock, and the first time I sat in it, it broke. I thought I
heard him say something about "wide load," but he swore
he'd said, "you hurt?" There was a snake in our town lake,
so I wouldn't swim even though the temperature was about
120°. Everyone was cranky because of the heat, but we
took turns sitting in Phoebe's old Care-Bears pool and
running through the sprinkler, so it wasn't so bad.

September

Martha celebrated the late summer harvest with an in-
depth study of the life and times of the humble potato. Of
course, by the time Martha is finished, nothing is humble.
Not even potato chips: Martha made Purple Peruvian
Waffled Potato Chips, using her trusty mandoline cutter.

And Yellow Finn Gratin. And Fingerlings steamed in butter.

Then, in what seemed like a surprise move to me, she segued into a bunch of traditional Mexican recipes to cook up and serve in a shady corner of the lawn. I've got a feeling you haven't lived until you've tried Pepita Brittle and Hibiscus Iced Tea.

We celebrated our late-summer harvest by picking the two pock-marked tomatoes that had survived the slugs, cut the roses that had survived the deer, and proudly displayed a zucchini from the garden that was only slightly smaller than our canoe. Then we went to the farmers' market and got stuff for dinner.

Phoebe went back to school and developed a facial tic that her pediatrician said was nerves (how nervous can you be in fifth grade?), Ollie stepped in the glue pots that we use to trap and maim mice and had to have most of his hair cut off, and we ate Mexican food straight out of the take-out tins in a shady corner of the garden.

October

Apples! Pies! Pumpkins! And a certain fixation on lamps. Martha's the girl you want if you ever need to make a lampshade, spruce up an old shade, rewire a lamp, gild a lampshade. Watts next? (Sorry!) The perfect pie! Martha pointed out that pie making has practically disap-

peared from our lives (oddly it never even appeared in mine) and she decided it was a tradition worth reviving. Martha revived Pumpkin Pie, Lemon Meringue Pie, and a Rustic Apple Tart baked in a cornmeal crust and served European style with Gorgonzola and a sprig of fresh lavender.

Dead leaves! Deer ticks! Jury duty! I actually made an Apple Crisp that was so good, I made it four more times in two weeks, until even Ollie wouldn't touch the stuff.

I discovered in my culinary forays that Frank Perdue was making his chicken nuggets in star and drumstick shapes, so I cooked them to a burnished gold in the toaster-oven and served them alternated on Phoebe's plate, European style, with ketchup and a dollop of Mott's applesauce.

November

Martha went to a potluck supper. Not just any potluck supper; the chefs and owners of five top Los Angeles restaurants brought their favorite impromptu dishes, if you can call Duck Lasagna or Shrimp in Kadaife Salad impromptu. And I don't want to be catty, but it didn't look like Martha brought anything, not even an impromptu Tuna Noodle Casserole.

Martha, in a philosophical aside, pointed out that some of the most interesting meals and dishes in American

history were born as potluck events, including Thanksgiving.

That must be true, because our Thanksgiving was definitely potluck. We wangled an invitation to my father- and stepmother-in-law's house in Connecticut. It was just us, Cousin Jimmy, Aunt Edith, and a very nice family of boat people that my in-laws had met at church, whom nobody knew were vegetarians. I brought an enormous bowl of my famous Brandied Cranberry Chutney, which took me hours to make, but everyone preferred the Ocean Spray.

December

"Caramel coated Seckel pears, antique iron urns piled high with citrus fruit, green persimmons, mercury glass globes, and weathered Christmas balls arranged in nests of bay leaves, silvered pomegranates, wild-mushroom-and-leek beggar's purses tied with leek ribbons and garnished with thyme, dried sycamore balls dressed in crinkle wire, loin of venison with red currant bordelaise sauce . . ." I'm sure Martha gilded a lily or two, but she didn't mention it. Why do I know that it must have snowed lightly on Christmas morning, that nobody spilled Château Talbot on the ecru linen tablecloth with the organza appliqué of reindeer, and that Martha's friends gave her presents such as eighteenth-century silk samplers and Chinese export-ware?

We ate another mail-order ham, I got a Dustbuster, a

bathrobe, and a book called *DOS for Dummies,* which was way too hard for me. Ollie absolutely refused to wear his brown felt reindeer ears, which he used to love. Then we all went ice-skating on the lake and pushed Ollie around in Phoebe's old ice sled. Did you ever see a dog smile?

Dear Phoebe,

It seems like only yesterday that I first heard that life-affirming, lusty scream in the delivery room of Mount Sinai Hospital, although on second thought, maybe that wasn't you — it might have been me reacting to forceps delivery with no medication after twenty-two hours of labor. Whatever. It was a big moment for both of us.

From the moment I first saw your cherubic little face, I had hopes and dreams for you. First of all, I hoped the little dent in your forehead from the forceps would go away. I hoped you wouldn't stay bald your whole life. I hoped you would figure out how to breast-feed so that you could teach me.

Now, ten years and two months later, you've got a full head of hair and no discernible dents. And I've still got wishes for you. I want you to be healthy and happy and kind and compassionate. I want you to know all the joy in life that comes from love and laughter, friends and family, hearth and home, sunsets and lilacs, puppies and babies, raindrops on roses and whiskers on kittens, bright copper kettles and warm woolen mittens. You could probably do without the copper kettles.

Yes, I've got all the normal hopes and dreams for you that any mother would have for her daughter. May you never get cellulite, have twins, be rejected by your safety school, have to sit in the center seat on a full 747, listen to your children sing "It's a Small World, After All" over and over on a long car trip.

I hope you'll always know *Goodnight Moon* by heart:

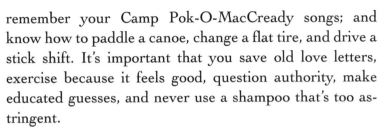

remember your Camp Pok-O-MacCready songs; and know how to paddle a canoe, change a flat tire, and drive a stick shift. It's important that you save old love letters, exercise because it feels good, question authority, make educated guesses, and never use a shampoo that's too astringent.

I want you to do whatever you can to save the whales, save the rain forest, protect endangered species, fight racism and sexism, help stamp out poverty and illiteracy, and make the world a better place. And if you happen to meet one of those cute, young Kennedy boys while you're doing it, that wouldn't be so terrible.

I'd like to think that you'll be the kind of person who gives up her seat on the bus to an older person. That you'll work in a soup kitchen or AIDS ward. That you won't put me and Daddy in the kind of nursing home where they make you dance the Hokey Pokey and wear those cellophane party hats with tight rubber bands under your chin on New Year's Eve.

Don't forget the maxims you grew up with at home: "Nobody's perfect," "Do unto others as you would have them do unto you," and "The one you touch is the one you take."

Be proud of your roots. Mommy's ancestors came from Russia and Sweden. On one side they were hardworking peasants in Kiev. On the other side they were hardworking peasants in Göteborg. Daddy's ancestors came from England and Ireland, where they were slightly more illus-

trious than Mommy's. Daddy's great-great-great-grandfather, George M. Dallas, was the eleventh vice president of the United States. One of Daddy's great-great-uncles built the first suspension bridge in Puerto Rico, although I don't know what he was doing there, since he lived in Dublin.

I hope you marry your best friend. I hope your children give you the same joy and satisfaction that you've given us.

What I hope most is that you remember how much we love and cherish you, bald, dented, and all.

ABOUT THE AUTHOR

Stephanie Pierson was born and raised in Baltimore, where she didn't know John Waters or Barry Levinson.

She went to Connecticut College and majored in Asian history. When she graduated she moved to New York, got a job as a copywriter for an advertising agency, and went out with all the wrong men in the tristate area.

Through some fluke, Stephanie met a terrific guy, married him, and gave birth to a daughter, Phoebe, whose shoe size has always roughly corresponded with her age. Phoebe is now ten and her shoe size is nine and a half.

Stephanie lives in New York, where she is a senior vice president, group creative director at Backer Spielvogel Bates. She is a contributing editor for *Metropolitan Home* magazine and has written for *Seven Days*, *McCall's*, *The New York Times*, and *New York* magazine.

Sometimes

WE

NEED

TRIALS

BOB SORGE

Oasis House
Kansas City, Missouri

Editor: Edie Mourey
Cover designer: Jessica Beedle
Typesetter: Dale Jimmo

ISBN: 978-1-937725-64-8

Stay connected with Bob at:
YouTube.com/bobsorge
Instagram: bob.sorge
Store: www.oasishouse.com
Blog: bobsorge.com
twitter.com/BOBSORGE
Facebook.com/BobSorgeMinistry

CONTENTS

1

PERSPECTIVE IS EVERYTHING

"Lord, I'm feeling the need for a fiery trial in my life right now. Please send me one." Prayed by nobody. Ever.

We don't ever feel like we need one, and yet from God's perspective we sometimes do. Stick around long enough and you'll likely encounter a fiery trial— because they're just part of the universal human experience. Furthermore, how we face them is one of the most important issues of life.

In a trial, perspective is *everything* because it determines how we face the trial. Perspective can be the difference between being a casualty or an overcomer.

For example, when on the cross, perspective was *everything* for Jesus. He knew Satan's diabolical design to tempt Him on the cross, and He knew the Father's good plan to change human history through the cross. It was His *knowledge* that enabled Him to complete His assignment (see Isa 53:11). Satan desperately wanted Jesus to enter into temptation (see Luke 22:46), but the Father prepared Jesus with the perspective He needed to finish the race with fullness of faith. That's why Jesus wasn't discouraged on the cross (see Isa 42:4)—He had His Father's perspective on the outcome of His sufferings.

Perspective is everything because it enables us to endure in our fiery trials until we obtain, by faith, God's intended outcome (see James 5:11).

There are two ways to look at your circumstances. You can view them through eyes of faith or through eyes of unbelief. To explain and illustrate my meaning, let's go to the example of the twelve spies who surveyed Canaan.

Twelve Spies

When the people of Israel came through the wilderness to the border of Canaan, Moses sent twelve men to spy out the land and bring back a report of what they found. Two of the spies (Caleb and Joshua) looked at Canaan with eyes of faith while the other ten looked at Canaan with eyes of unbelief. What they saw was starkly divergent.

As we're about to see, unbelief rewrites the narrative.

When the ten unbelieving spies brought their report to the children of Israel, they said, "We are not able to go up against the people" (Num 13:31). They told the Israelites that they saw fortified cities and giant champions. They added, "The land through which we have gone as spies is a land that devours its inhabitants" (Num 13:32).

What a curious statement. Why would they describe Canaan as *a land that devours its inhabitants?* Because they had seen an uncommon number of funerals in their travels. There were funerals *everywhere.* And it wasn't just the elderly who were dying. Rather, the Canaanites were burying young men in their prime. The spies wondered, *Why are so many young, strong Canaanites dying premature deaths?* The ten looked at the funerals with eyes of unbelief and concluded, "This land devours its inhabitants."

They were saying to the people of Israel, "Canaan is a hostile country. If we settle in this land, it will devour and kill us. God has set us up for slaughter."

Unbelief had distorted their vision.

In contrast, Caleb and Joshua surveyed the land of Canaan with eyes of faith. They saw the same thing the others saw—funerals everywhere—but they saw them from a different perspective. In their report to the people of Israel, Caleb and Joshua said, "Their protection has departed from them, and the LORD is with us. Do not fear them" (Num. 14:9).

In other words, Caleb and Joshua were saying, "God has removed the protection of the Canaanites and is thinning their ranks. He has gone before us and is already fighting on our behalf."

I can imagine them reminding the people of Israel, "Don't you remember that God said He would cut them off? He promised that He would send hornets before us and cause our enemies to turn their backs to us.[1] God is fulfilling His promises and is preparing the way before us. He's weakening our enemies!"

Faith had given them clear vision.

Eyes of Faith

All twelve spies looked at the exact same circumstances (funerals everywhere), but eyes of faith had a profoundly different conclusion from eyes of unbelief.

Eyes of unbelief said, "God is against us," but eyes of faith said, "God is for us!"

Eyes of unbelief said, "This is horrible," but eyes of faith said, "This is awesome!"

Eyes of unbelief said, "We're doomed for failure," but eyes of faith said, "We're set up for victory!"

Eyes of unbelief said, "We've got to turn around," but eyes of faith said, "It's time to march forward!"

Eyes of unbelief said, "God is trying to destroy us," but eyes of faith said, "God is giving us our inheritance."

We want eyes like Caleb and Joshua—eyes of faith—so we can see our trials from God's perspective! When we get God's perspective on our circumstances, it changes *everything*. We see things that others around us don't see.

1   See Exod 23:23–28.

As you work your way through this short book, ask God to give you His perspective on your circumstances. When you see your trial through His eyes, your confidence in Him will grow, and you'll receive strength to lay hold of His good purpose for your life.

Necessary Trials

There are two ways to look at your fiery trial. You can look at it through eyes of unbelief and grow in anxiety and dread; or you can look at it with eyes of faith and grow in confidence that God will fulfill His promises.

Now, I totally get it—we don't like trials. We don't want them, and we don't enjoy them. Nor do I think we should ask for them. But the truth is, sometimes we need them.

Unbelief rewrites the narrative

"But didn't Christ lift us above all the troubles of life," I imagine someone arguing, "when He blessed us, as it says in Ephesians 1:3, with every spiritual blessing in the heavenlies? Why would we need fiery trials when Jesus said in John 10:10 that He came to give us life more abundantly?"

Great question! Fiery trials certainly seem contradictory, at first glance, to the more abundant life Jesus promised. But maybe we have a wrong idea about the blessed life.

Sometimes we imagine the blessed life to look like a blissful YouTube commercial that portrays financial prosperity, excellent health, fulfilling relationships, and delightful distractions. But a blessed life is not a trial-free life.

A trial-free life doesn't leave us enhanced and enriched. Rather, it makes us soft, self-centered, slothful, and sluggish.

What does the blessed life look like? It's a life that forges forward, despite resistance, and develops godly character in the struggle. The blessed life has received grace to persevere in faith through trials and ultimately sits with Christ on His throne as an overcomer in love (see Rev 3:21).

If we're to grow into that kind of faith and love, then fiery trials will inevitably be *necessary*.

God, What Are You Thinking?

When we fall into a fiery trial, our "spirit makes diligent search" (Ps 77:6). Like David in Psalm 77, we claw for answers and search for God's perspective. *Why did this happen? What did I do wrong? God, what are You seeing and thinking?*

We want to know both the *what* and the *when* (see 1 Pet 1:11). That is, we want to know *what* God is doing in our lives, and *when* He'll act on our behalf. *God, what are You doing in my situation? When are You going to fulfill Your promise and answer my prayer?*

The questions cascade like endless torrents. *God, what are You thinking? What do You see? What is Your purpose? Why have You allowed this to happen to me? What is Satan's agenda in all this? What do I need to learn from this? What should I do now? How is this going to end?*

Bottom line, we want God's perspective on our circumstances. But instead of answering our questions all at once, He usually invites us into a journey of ever-increasing faith. The journey is profoundly transformational. Hear it carefully: Nothing is more life-transforming than faith that endures through fiery trials (see James 1:2–4).

You Needed This One

When it comes to fiery trials, God sees things very differently from us. We get mired sometimes in our circumstances, but He sits enthroned above it all. We don't know where the journey is leading, but He sees the end from the beginning. We don't understand all His purposes, but He knows the good plans He has for us (see Jer 29:11).

How different is God's perspective from ours? He said it this way:

> *"For My thoughts are not your thoughts, nor are your ways My ways," says the LORD. "For as the heavens are higher than the earth, so are My ways higher than your ways, and My thoughts than your thoughts" (Isa 55:8–9).*

That's God's way of saying, "I don't view anything the way you do." We're often stuck in a myopic, earthly outlook, but He sees our trials from a heavenly, eternal perspective.

Trials. Sometimes we'd rather talk about something else, but this topic is so foundational to the Christian life that Paul, James, and Peter all began their epistles talking about trials (2 Cor 1:4–11; James 1:2–4; 1 Pet 1:6–7). When we're in them, nothing is more important than gaining God's perspective on them.

When we fall into a fiery trial, sometimes we respond by going, *I don't need this right now*. But God's perspective is different. He's thinking, *Actually, you do. You needed this one.*

Why would we sometimes need trials? Well, to get God's perspective on this question, let's go to the ultimate source—the bastion and fountainhead of all wisdom. Let's go to the cross of Christ.

2
THE CROSS WAS NECESSARY

After His resurrection, Jesus appeared to His disciples on several occasions and left them with some final instructions before ascending to His Father in heaven. His directives were mostly forward-looking and vision-casting regarding the Great Commission that lay before them. But the cross was such a huge event that Jesus took time in His visits with the disciples to look back and debrief with them about it.

The first time He reflected on His cross was on the afternoon of His resurrection as He walked the Emmaus road with two disciples. He said to them:

Ought not the Christ to have suffered these things and to enter into His glory? (Luke 24:26).

With the words *ought not*, His message to them was simply this: The Christ's sufferings were *necessary*.

The second time He debriefed on His cross was just a few hours later. It was the Sunday evening of His resurrection, and the eleven disciples were huddled in a Jerusalem house with some of their friends. Jesus suddenly appeared in the room and had this to say about His cross:

> *Thus it is written, and thus it was necessary for the Christ to suffer and to rise from the dead the third day (Luke 24:46).*

He reiterated the same message: His sufferings were *necessary*.

Our English translation veils the fact that He used the same word, in both instances, to characterize His cross. To see the linguistic repetition, we must look at the original Greek text.

When Jesus said, "Ought not" in verse 26 and "it was necessary" in verse 46, He used the same word. In the original text, it's the Greek word *dei*. In verse 26, *dei* is translated *ought*, and in verse 46, it's translated *necessary*. The meaning of *dei* in both verses is identical.

Strong's Exhaustive Concordance defines *dei* as *it is necessary*.[1] Zodhiates describes it as *necessary by the nature of things; must; intrinsic necessity; an unavoidable, urgent, compulsory necessity*.[2]

Both times that Jesus looked back at the cross, He

1   G1163 – dei. James Strong, The New Strong's Exhaustive Concordance of the Bible (Nashville, TN: Thomas Nelson Publishers, 1990).

2   Spiros Zodhiates, *The Complete WordStudy New Testament* (Chattanooga, TN: AMG International; 1992).

spoke of it as *necessary*. That was just about the only thing He had to say about it. In fact, He said the same thing about the cross even before it happened. During His three-year teaching ministry, Jesus used *dei* a number of times, but He used it especially when speaking of His upcoming sufferings.[3] For example, *dei* is translated *must* in this verse: "And He began to teach them that the Son of Man *must* suffer many things, and be rejected by the elders and chief priests and scribes, and be killed, and after three days rise again" (Mark 8:31).

Both before and after His sufferings, Jesus made it very clear: *The cross was necessary*.

What Jesus Didn't Say

Consider for a moment what He *didn't* say about the cross. He didn't say, "That was the greatest injustice of human history—it should have never happened!" True, it was the greatest injustice of human history, but yet it *had* to happen. If we really understood that, it would probably change how we view some of today's injustices. Instead of demanding a tribunal of accountability for all the injustices we observe sinners committing, we might come to perceive the injustices of our world as sometimes being necessary vehicles for God's purposes to be fulfilled.

Jesus *didn't* say, "Pilate really blew that one! His

3 See Matt 16:21; 26:54; Mark 8:31; Luke 9:22; 13:33; 17:25; 22:37; John 3:14; 12:34.

wife warned him, but the man wouldn't listen. And the chief priests? They're going to regret that one big time! Just wait till Judgment Day and see how they fare." He didn't talk about the way the leaders sinned against Him.

Jesus *didn't* say, "The devil really came after Me. He raged against Me and tried to take Me out. And just when his attack was the most fierce, all you guys abandoned Me. Where were you at crunch time? You said you were willing to die with Me, but then, when I needed you most, you disap-peared." No, Jesus didn't talk about Satan's agenda at the cross—even though Satan clearly had one. Nor did He speak of His disciples' failures. He wasn't mindful of Satan's agency or man's agency, but only of God's agency at the cross.

Your trial is your certification

Here's what Jesus *was* saying:

"I *had* to do the cross—to fulfill Scripture."

"I *had* to do the cross—to complete all righteousness."

"I *had* to do the cross—to destroy the devil."

"I *had* to do the cross—to overcome sin, hell, and the grave."

"I *had* to do the cross—to purchase your redemption."

"I *had* to do the cross—to heal your infirmities."

"I *had* to do the cross—to become a faithful High Priest."

"I *had* to do the cross—to earn My stripes as the Captain of your salvation."

In light of God's eternal plan to redeem humanity, Jesus was saying that *the cross was necessary*.

Peter Used the Same Word

When Peter wrote about fiery trials in his first epistle, he also used the Greek word *dei*. I've italicized its occurrence so you can see it:

> *In this you greatly rejoice, though now for a little while, if need be, you have been grieved by various trials, that the genuineness of your faith, being much more precious than gold that perishes, though it is tested by fire, may be found to praise, honor, and glory at the revelation of Jesus Christ (1 Pet 1:6–7).*

The Greek word *dei* is present in the phrase *if need be*. A literal rendering would read *if being necessary*. Peter was literally saying, "Sometimes trials are necessary."

By using *dei*—the same word Jesus used to describe His sufferings—Peter was drawing a straight line between the cross and our fiery trials. He was indicating that our sufferings in our fiery trials are directly connected to Jesus' sufferings on the cross. Peter was inferring, *just as it was necessary for Jesus to suffer on the cross, sometimes it's also necessary for us to suffer fiery trials.*

This connecting line Peter drew between the cross and our trials is the same line Paul drew when he wrote, "I now rejoice in my sufferings for you, and fill up in my flesh what is lacking in the afflictions of Christ, for the sake of His body, which is the church" (Col 1:24). For years I've wondered, *What does it mean to fill up in our flesh what is lacking in the afflictions of Christ?* The answer is coming into focus: *It means to endure fiery trials that test our faith.*

Just as the cross was a fiery trial that tested Jesus' faith, your point of suffering is a fiery trial that is testing your faith.

Some people will likely look at your difficulty and say to you, "This isn't right. This should have never happened to you." But from God's perspective, it's the trial that's making you who you are. It's producing in you more fruit to God than ever. It's revealing God's redemption in your family. It's giving God room to write a great story with your life.

Your trial is your certification (1 Pet 1:6–7). The way you walk through it demonstrates to heaven and earth that your faith is authentic.

On the final day, when we're standing before the throne, I imagine the question being asked, "Is this person's faith genuine?" And then I also imagine the answer. "Look at her faith! She had circumstances against her, finances against her, Satan against her, hell against her, temptation against her, her flesh against her, the world against her, people against her, her health against her, even family and friends against her. And yet, look how she stood. She never backed down. She praised You when heaven was silent. She loved You when she couldn't see You or feel You. This is the real deal. This is true faith."

And I imagine heaven placing its official imprimatur—Seal of Authenticity—on the service of your faith. *Certified and approved!*

When your faith is certified authentic before the throne, it will "be found to praise, honor, and glory at the revelation of Jesus Christ" (1 Pet 1:7). The praise, however, won't be going to *you*. They won't be saying to you, "Way to go! You were awesome out there! You ran a great race!"

Instead, they'll be glorifying God's grace in your life. They'll say things like, "Look what His grace has accomplished in you! You were so feeble, so prone to wander, so vulnerable to temptation, so wavering in your faith. But His grace was up to the challenge! He perfected your faith in spite of your weakness! Look what God has done!"

The crowning glory of our story will be the fact that Christ alone will be praised and honored for our faith.

Peter said this kind of faith is *much more precious than gold that perishes* (1 Pet 1:7). It's *incorruptible*

(1 Pet 1:4). How can we gain a faith that's so much more valuable and priceless than gold? There's really only one way—through fiery trials.

To gain faith *this* precious, sometimes we *need* trials in our lives.

3
TEST THE THING

Virtually every product available for purchase on the market today has been tested. Before a company releases a new product for the public to purchase, they'll test it to ensure it produces the desired effect. Until it's tested, they can't know for sure that it meets their standards of quality.

Car manufacturers, for example, always test their vehicles before releasing them to the public. If a vehicle fails one of their performance tests, manufacturers don't automatically discard that model of car and start all over; rather, they improve its design until that model satisfactorily passes the test.

The same is true for us. When God tests us, He's not looking for an excuse to toss us aside, but to prepare us for greater service.

For example, when Peter failed the test at Jesus' trial and denied Him three times, Jesus didn't dispense with him and look for a replacement, Rather, He used the failure to draw Peter higher. Jesus knew that Peter couldn't repent of something he didn't see, so Jesus used the test, in His kindness, to show Peter his personal bankruptcy. In tears of repentance, Peter cried to God for help. Through it all, Jesus released grace to Peter and made him an even more fruitful servant in the kingdom. Peter's failure was actually an important part of His process of preparation.

A Test Reveals True Colors

Sometimes you don't know what you've got until you test the thing.

For example, suppose you visit a local car dealer because you want to buy a car. As your eyes scan the vehicles that are sitting in the lot, you spot a car that grabs your interest. You like the color, model, features, and specifications, and you can even live with the sticker price. But before you buy it, you have an important question for the sales rep. "Could I take the car for a test drive?"

Why? Because you don't really know what the car is like until you test it.

This principle is true in many areas of life. The nature or quality of some things in life can't be fully known until they're tested. Here's a couple more examples.

Character is not known until it's proven by temptation. An entire book could be written on that statement. You don't really know how reliable someone's character is in a certain area until they encounter the perfect temptation. They might say, "I would never steal," but then watch what happens when the planets align and an idyllic set of temptations suddenly unfolds before them. What if no one would ever know? What if it were impossible for them to get caught? Would they still refuse to steal? In the presence of the perfect temptation, the nature of their character will come to light because *temptation reveals character*.

In a similar way, *love is not known until it's proven by hatred*. We might suppose that we love everybody in the world unconditionally—until they move in next door to us. Now, when we encounter irrational, unprovoked hatred, we find the purity of our love being challenged. Does their hatred vaporize our love? Hostility and venom have a way of revealing the true nature of love.

Faith is not known until it's proven by trials

In the same way, *faith is not known until it's proven by trials*. Some of us might feel fairly confident about our faith, but how firmly will our faith stand when we suddenly fall into a grievous trial? Fiery trials have a built-in way of revealing the true nature of our faith.

Sometimes we need trials in our lives so that our faith can be tested, strengthened, and confirmed.

Are Trials a Blessing?

I can imagine a cynic being a little bit critical of my point here, pushing back on it and saying, "Well, if trials are such a great blessing to you, Bob, may you be *baptized* with them! May you be blessed with more!"

I totally get this objection. My critics think I'm being inconsistent. On the one hand, they suppose me saying that trials are helpful blessings in our lives, but on the other hand, I don't really want them. It's a great objection, so let me answer it with this: *Trials are not a blessing*.

Why not? Because when God blesses us, "The blessing of the LORD makes one rich, and He adds no sorrow with it" (Prov 10:22). Blessings come with no sorrow. When He's blessing you with provision, protection, healing, wisdom, understanding, or peace, His blessings come with no sorrow. Trials, on the other hand, come with *many* sorrows. Trials, therefore, are not blessings.

It's not a blessing, it's a trial.

But trials can culminate in great blessing if we respond properly to them. When we come through trials victoriously, they open to some of the greatest attainments in the kingdom of God: eternal fruit, godly character, beautiful holiness, and mighty exploits. Never waste a good trial. Squeeze from it all the refined gold that you possibly can!

Trials can lead to great blessing in the end, but even so, I don't suggest that you ask for trials. I think it's better to pray, "Do not lead us into temptation" (Matt 6:13). That's a prayer of humility. That prayer from Jesus is a recognition that our strength is small and apart from His empowering grace our flesh will repeatedly fail in the fight with temptation. We don't want to be tempted with anything that could lead us into sin. Rather, we ask to be delivered from the evil one.

Don't ask for trials. In other words, don't ask to be pruned, chastened, refined, or sifted by God. Instead, ask for blessings. Ask for big blessings, and then trust Him to answer in the best way.

Dangerous Prayers

So I don't really believe in asking for trials. But I do believe in praying dangerous prayers. What are dangerous prayers? The kind of prayers that are so trusting in God's goodness that they give God a blank slate to write the story of our lives His way.

We sing some pretty dangerous songs in our churches. When you consider the lyrics, you have to wonder if we really understand some of the things we sing to God. "Fire of God, consume me." "Take all of me, I'm Yours." "I give myself away." Maybe we don't always understand all the implications of some of our lyrics, but I'm still over here saying, sing the dangerous song.

What is the dangerous prayer? Okay, I'm going to tell you. Here it is: *Whatever it takes*.

That's the dangerous prayer because it's willing to pay any price in order to enter into kingdom fullness.

"I've got to have You, God—whatever it takes."

"I've got to know You, Jesus—whatever it takes."

"I've got to see You, Jesus—whatever it takes."

"I've got to be closer, Lord—whatever it takes."

That prayer is so lovesick that it hands Jesus a blank check. It says to Jesus, "I invite You to do whatever it takes to get me where I need to be. I can't get there on my own, so I surrender fully to Your leadership in my life. I know that the path You choose will be perfect. I'm confident in Your goodness, mercy, and grace. Do whatever it takes, but give me more of You!"

The reason it's a dangerous prayer is because sometimes the path He chooses can lead us through a fiery trial. But to get to some destinations in the heart of God, we actually *need* trials.

4

TRIALS REFRESH OUR FRAGRANCE

One reason we sometimes need trials in our lives is because of the way they refresh our fragrance before God. Here's the Scripture that opens this for us:

> Moab has been at ease from his youth; he has settled on his dregs, and has not been emptied from vessel to vessel, nor has he gone into captivity. Therefore his taste remained in him, and his scent has not changed (Jer 48:11).

In this verse, God explained why judgment would be coming to the nation of Moab. He likened Moab to a vat of wine. In the winemaking process, a winemaker will pour wine from one vessel to another. Why? Because the winemaker wants to separate the wine from the sediment that has settled at the bottom of the vessel. When the wine is poured into another vessel, the dregs are left behind and can then be discarded. With the dregs removed, the wine can continue forward in the fining and clarifying process.

You don't want to let wine sit on its lees indefinitely

lest the wine become gritty and the flavor unpleasant.

God pictured Moab as a vessel of wine, and said the nation had never been emptied from one vessel to another. It would have been helpful if they had been temporarily taken in captivity to another country. But no, nothing had ever happened to them to pour them out, get them off their dregs, and refresh their fragrance. Instead, they had just lazed on their lees—stale, stagnant, and stinking. The entire nation had become distasteful to God. Their fusty fragrance would incur divine judgment.

> *When we're comfortable for too long, it never ends well*

Did you know that nations have a fragrance to God? I wonder what America smells like to God. I wonder what my birthplace, Canada, smells like to God. Do you wonder what your nation smells like to God?

Churches have a fragrance to God.

Families have a fragrance to God.

Individuals have a fragrance to God.

Sometimes it's good to ask the question, *What do I smell like to God?* Is the fragrance of my love fresh and inviting to Him, or stale and unchanged?

When our lives get settled and stagnant, sometimes He'll pour us from one vessel to another. We rarely enjoy that process because it's usually very disruptive to our routines and lifestyle. But in one sense, isn't that the point? He'll intentionally disrupt our comforts so that we'll be dislodged from the overly-familiar and be freshened in our fragrance.

Haven't you noticed? Any time you get comfortable for too long, it never ends well.

The Holy Spirit has been given to comfort us but not to make us comfortable. The comfortable become curdled. When we get comfortable we stop growing because growth almost always proceeds from discomfort.

Through Jeremiah 48:11, God was basically saying, "If I don't empty you from vessel to vessel, you'll get soft, flabby, settled, stagnant, and sluggish."

God looks at some of us and thinks, *You've been living in the same house, on the same street, in the same city, going to the same school, working the same job, hanging with the same friends, watching the same shows, playing the same video games, and going to the same church—for too long. We're going to mix this up.*

Suddenly, you find yourself being emptied from one vessel to another. Everything in your life is shaken and rearranged. Nothing seems predictable, and you can't find your equilibrium. *What was that? What just happened to me?* Maybe it was a hospitalization or a move, or an unexpected change of career, or a bankruptcy, or something else that was painfully life-altering.

You become desperate for understanding, so you cry out, "God, what are You doing in my life?"

His answer seems to be, "Freshening you up."

Go ahead and take a closer look at your life now. You've got fresh zeal, fresh fire, and fresh longing. You weep again when you read the word. You're lovesick for Jesus all over again. You're kind again with people and gracious with your words. In other words, your fragrance before God has been renewed.

Be honest about it. You actually *needed* this trial.

5

SOMETIMES WE NEED STORMS

Storms are destructive forces of nature, but did you know they also accomplish some positive things in the world? "What positive things?" someone might wonder. Well, let me mention some of the plusses. When you see them, you'll probably agree that our planet actually needs storms.

Here are some of the benefits of storms. For starters, they bring rainfall to places in desperate need of water. They flush groundwater and surface water, and help rivers discharge their accrued waste. They replenish lakes and underground aquifers. They regulate Earth's temperatures by equalizing our planet's heat. They nourish the teeming creatures of the seas by dragging nutrients into the ocean. They clear air pollution. They build barrier beaches and renew the land mass of islands. They renew forests by leveling diseased or weak trees. When storms discharge lightning, they renew the gasses of the ozone.

Yes, the Earth needs storms.

I live in Kansas City, Missouri, USA, and they use an expression here, *a hundred-year storm*. The term applies to a storm that is so unusually intense that you'll see a storm of that ferocity perhaps every hundred years or so. These storms are rare, but when they hit, they'll do unanticipated damage because of the unprecedented flooding that accompanies them. For example, Kansas City has experienced two such storms since records were kept—in 1844 and 1951. The flooding was catastrophic and photos of the devastation may be viewed easily with an internet search.

When property developers bring their building plans before zoning boards in this part of the country, one of the questions they always ask is, "Are you looking to build a structure in a hundred-year flood zone?" If they determine that the building would sit in a flood plain, they probably won't let you build it. The house might sit safely enough for several decades, but one of these years a storm is likely to move through the area that will flood the house and produce severe structural damage.

Storms sometimes cause rivers to cut new channels. For example, here in Missouri, there are portions of the Missouri River that flow in channels that are a half-mile or more from places where the river once flowed. What would cause a river to be redirected that significantly? Storms.

Similar things can happen in our lives, as it says in

Proverbs 21:1, "The king's heart is in the hand of the LORD, like the rivers of water; He turns it wherever He wishes." When a hundred-year storm sweeps through our lives, it will flood over the channels of everything once familiar to us and cut entirely new channels in our hearts and our patterns of living. After a hundred-year storm, our lives probably won't return to what they once were. Some things will be lost, but in some cases, the storm can actually be a divine mercy because of the new vistas that open.

Storms don't bother Jesus. They may unsettle us, but they don't threaten Him. He relaxes in storms (see Matt 8:24). Jesus is used to living in a place where there is incessant thunder and lightning (see Rev 4:5). As the warden of the winds, He's the Master of your storm!

Trees need wind so their branches flex rather than snap

The Biosphere

In the remote desert town of Oracle, Arizona, there's a world-famous tourist trap called Biosphere 2. It's a huddled grove of half-globe buildings that stands out starkly against the surrounding desert topography. It's the largest greenhouse system ever built.

The entire venture was a speculative scientific

experiment and was obviously funded by someone with lots of money. The venture actually had to do with space exploration.

The question was this: Could a self-contained ecosystem be built that could support and sustain human life independently of the surrounding environment? If it could be operationally successful in the desert, the next question was whether they could copy/paste the ecosystem, place it on Mars, and establish an outpost that could support human life.

The experiment went bad, but it still attracts tourists from around the world.

Somebody once said, "I wonder what would happen if we planted fruit trees in this Biosphere." In the enclosed greenhouse, every aspect of the fruit trees' habitat could be controlled. The trees could be given perfect lighting, perfect temperatures, perfect irrigation, and perfect fertilization. What would happen if fruit trees were nursed in ideal growing conditions?

They decided to give it a try. And sure enough, the trees produced a bountiful harvest—with only one problem. The branches of the trees kept snapping under the weight of the fruit.

Why? Because there was no wind in the Biosphere's enclosed, artificial environment. Wind keeps branches flexible. In the absence of wind, branches become inflexible and brittle. Then, under the weight of the harvest, the branches snap and break. On the downside, wind stresses and sometimes even damages limbs; but on the upside, it keeps them flexible and pliant.

Trees actually *need* wind. Wind forces branches to remain flexible, and then when they're bearing the weight of a vigorous harvest, they bend rather than break. Healthy fruit trees need stormy winds, therefore, so they can be fruitful and productive in time of harvest.

The same is sometimes true for us. None of us enjoys when stormy winds hit our lives, and yet they're sometimes necessary.

The winds keep us flexible so we can sustain the fruit of our next season in God.

It's true. You've *needed* this storm.

6

STRESSED VINES PRODUCE VINTAGE WINES

I once watched a winemaking documentary in which the narrators were describing the factors that produce a vintage wine. A vintage wine, as I understand it, is a wine from a particular growing season that has exceptional flavor because of the growing conditions that year.

Folks will talk about a vintage wine for years. "2012. That was the year. Try to get yourself a bottle from 2012. They're pretty hard to find, and you'll pay for it, but if you can find a bottle from 2012—"

When it comes to winemaking, I'm a novice, but as I watched the documentary, I thought to myself, *I know what produces a vintage wine. You just need lots of sunlight, lots of precipitation, lots of warmth, and VOILA, you've got yourself a vintage wine.* But the winemakers said it's exactly the opposite.

To get a vintage wine, they said, you must have a *hard* growing season. You need adversarial conditions that force the vines to work extra hard. Too much sun.

Not enough sun. Too much rain. Not enough rain. Too much cold. When vines are stressed by adversarial weather conditions and have to work harder than usual to produce a crop, that's where you get a vintage wine. The harvest will likely be smaller in volume, but the flavor of the wine can be uncommonly delightful.

They said, *You'll never get a vintage wine from unstressed vines.*

Drought Irrigation

They went on to say that, in times of drought, a farmer won't irrigate his vineyard. As a novice, my response was like, "Bro! That's *exactly* when you need to irrigate your vineyard. Hello! There's no rain! Save your harvest from total loss and irrigate your vineyard."

But they said no. In a drought, a farmer will intentionally stress the vines by withholding irrigation. Why? Because if he irrigates his vineyard during a drought, the roots of the vines will return to the surface to capture the surface moisture. But if he intentionally stresses the vines by withholding irrigation, the roots of the vines have only one direction to go.

Now, under the duress of drought, the vines become desperate to survive. In that fight for survival, the vines channel their strength into the roots and begin to push their roots deeper into the soil than ever before. The plants thrust their rootlets into crevices, crannies, and depths in the soil they've never before reached.

For the *Star Trek* fans out there, the roots are now going where no root has gone before.

Did you know that soil gets tired? Soil gets depleted. Roots tap the nutrients in soil, and, as season follows season, the vigor of the soil becomes increasingly depleted.

But as the vine, in its desperate pursuit of moisture, forces its roots deeper than ever before, those new roots come into contact with untapped minerals and untouched nutrients. When the roots absorb these full-bodied nutrients, *that's* where you get a vintage wine.

Stressed vines produce vintage wines.

If your life is to produce a vintage wine for the delight and pleasure of your beloved Lord Jesus, then maybe this stressful season you've been in has been *necessary*. Maybe you've needed this drought. You've probably wondered if you would survive this famine, but is it possible you would have never put roots this deeply into God unless you had been driven to holy desperation?

Look what holy desperation has driven you to! You're fasting more than ever; you're devouring the word of God in every spare moment; you're journaling the things He's speaking to you; you're hearing His voice more clearly than you've heard in a long time;

you're learning what it means to abide in Christ; you're being filled with the Holy Spirit every day; you're receiving life from others in the body of Christ; you're giving more spiritual life to others than ever before.

As you're accessing fresh nutrients in the word and Spirit, God is crafting a vintage wine with your life. He's redeeming your drought! You thought the trial would take you out, but instead, your faith is being strengthened, and the wine of your love is delighting His heart.

You actually *needed* this drought so that you would put down roots this deeply.

Joseph's Drought

When I think about how God sometimes causes us to push our roots deeper into Him, I'm reminded of Joseph's prison. To Joseph, his prison felt like a drought, but it forced him to thrust his roots deeper into God. As painful as it was, I want to suggest he actually *needed* that prison in order to become the man God was shaping. Let me explain.

Joseph was an exceptionally talented young man. He had people skills, communication skills, leadership skills, administrative skills, business skills, accounting skills, entrepreneurial instincts, problem-solving abilities, a quick mind, creative ingenuity, charm and charisma, and on top of it all, a buff body. The guy was a package, and everything he touched turned to gold.

But as capable was Joseph was, he wasn't capable enough to meet the challenge of God's high call on his life. His skills could only take him so far. To steward the destiny of his call, he needed to find a source that went deeper than his gifts and talents. In other words, he needed to learn to live from his spirit.

Prison made Joseph desperate. He was like, "I'm going to *die* here!" He had no advocate to plead his case or family member in town to bail him out. Facing a life sentence in a hell hole, he became a desperate man—desperate, that is, to break free of his prison.

In his desperation, he knew it was pointless to exercise his strengths and talents because his natural abilities were powerless to get him out of prison. The only direction he knew to go was deep into the Holy Spirit.

Twenty-year-old men aren't typically in touch with their spirit. They function more from their mind, muscles, and moxie. But God wanted to train Joseph to serve from his spirit, hence the prison. God shut down Joseph's natural strengths so that he would be forced to find spiritual strength.

Like a vine in a drought, Joseph tenaciously pushed the roots of his spirit deeper into God than he ever had before. He chased after God with the desperation of a dying man.

Deeper

I can hear Joseph saying, "God, I don't get You! I've

been faithful to You, loving You, serving You, and living in Your presence. But serving You doesn't work. All that my faithful service has done is land me in this horrible prison."

And all God said was, "Deeper."

"God, I've held to Your promises. You promised things to my great-grandfather Abraham that I cherish and treasure. But holding to Your promises obviously isn't working in my life."

And God persisted, "Deeper."

Identify your God language, study it, and master it

"But I've separated myself, God, from my wayward generation. I even said no to Potiphar's wife. And look where my integrity has gotten me. I'm rotting in a sewer! Clearly, serving You doesn't work."

And God just kept saying, "Deeper. Go deeper, son."

Dream Interpretation

Desperate to understand God's intention in the prison, Joseph began to reach into the depths of the Holy Spirit more fervently than he had in all his life. He had always been a man of prayer, but this was different. This was the frantic clawing of a man desperate to breathe.

In his pursuit of God's heart, he decided to study his God language. Joseph's God language was dreams. In other words, God spoke to Joseph through dreams. When he was younger, God had given him two divine dreams that were clear and extraordinarily compelling. Now, in his prison, he was desperate to know what those dreams meant. He couldn't reconcile the hope of his dreams with the hopelessness of his prison. The dreams seemed to indicate greatness, but his prison screamed, "You're dead!"

God, what did those dreams mean?

Joseph devoted himself in the Holy Spirit to studying dream interpretation. He became a student of his God language, and good thing he did! When the butler and baker came to prison and received divine dreams, Joseph was able to interpret their dreams (see Gen 40). Then, when Pharaoh received a divine dream, he was able to interpret Pharaoh's dream (see Gen 41).

Joseph didn't get out of prison because of his multifarious gift set; he got out of prison because he had cultivated an inner life in God. He made room for the Spirit of God to live inside him, giving him illumination and understanding (see Gen 41:38–39). In one moment, he went from the prison to the palace—because he had gone deep in God and studied his God language.

What's Your God Language?

That's a great question to ask. In other words, ask yourself, *How does God talk to me?* Too often we get distracted by how He *doesn't* talk to us. Too often we wonder things like, *Why doesn't God talk to me in the same way He talks to my pastor?* That's the wrong question. Stop looking at how God talks to others, and focus instead on how He talks to you. In other words, stop obsessing about how He *doesn't* talk to you, and look instead at how He *does*.

God will come alongside, match the cadence of your stride, and walk with you in a way that's unique to just the two of you. Become skillful in your cadence with God.

God talks to people in all sorts of ways, according to their unique personality and personhood. He'll likely talk to you differently from the way He talks to your neighbor. God talks to some people through dreams. With others, He talks to them through nature. With many, He talks to them primarily through Scripture. With some, He talks to them through inner impressions. For others, it may happen during quiet listening.

What's your God language? Identify it, study it, and master it. Mastering your God language just might get you out of prison, too.

Through the confinement of prison, Joseph found

a depth in God he would have never otherwise discovered. He found a realm that isn't accessed by natural strengths, gifts, or talents. It's a dimension that is, "'Not by might nor by power, but by My Spirit,' says the LORD of hosts" (Zech 4:6).

Joseph needed that depth in God so that he could lead the nation of Egypt through a blistering seven-year famine and earn the relational authority with Pharaoh to establish his family in prosperity in the land of Goshen. Prison was necessary to fashion Joseph into the world leader that God needed. In the end, he saved every soul in the nation of Egypt and became a feeder of nations.

When Joseph put deeper roots into God, here's some of the fruit that came forth: meekness, compassion, selflessness, wisdom, discernment, and profound Spirit dependence. Prison forced Joseph to find and live from his spirit. Again, he didn't get out of prison because of his winsome strengths but because he learned to connect with the Holy Spirit.

Simeon

Joseph's brother, Simeon, also needed prison. That's why Joseph imprisoned Simeon for an extended period of time (see Gen 42:24). It was a gesture of mercy, to give Simeon an opportunity to face the dark places in his soul, repent, and come out a better man. Genesis 49:5–7 would seem to hint, however, that Simeon wasn't changed by his prison in the same way Joseph was. Simeon was offered the same opportunity as Joseph, and even though he needed the prison, he wasn't able to surrender to its excavations.

The prison that makes one person bitter makes another person better.

To produce a vintage wine with Joseph's life, God had to take him through the drought of prison. Might the same be true for you? Is it possible you've actually *needed* this drought in your life?

May you never forget it. Stressed vines produce vintage wines.

7

A TOWERING TESTIMONY

When God wants to construct a towering testimony with your life, trials become foundationally necessary for that kind of testimony. Let me explain what I mean.

Some testimonies are towering while others are more modest. Said another way, some life stories have greater significance than others. Paul pointed to this when he said that one star differs from another in glory (see 1 Cor 15:41). He meant that one star in the sky will shine more brightly than another. In context, he was speaking of the glory that our lives will display in eternity. The stories of some believers will shine with greater glory than those of others. That's true for the stories of biblical characters, and it's also true for stories of believers today.

For example, Peter's story in Scripture shines as a very bright star, and by comparison, Rhoda's story shines much more modestly. If someone would ask, "Who is Rhoda?" their question would underscore my point. Very little is known about her, and few even recognize her name. The place that her life and story has found in history is much more obscure and dim than Peter's.

Paul used the metaphor of stars differing from one another in glory, but in this chapter I want to use the metaphor of towers differing from one another in grandeur. Just as Peter's testimony towered much higher than Rhoda's in the Bible, I want to consider how towers differ from one another in height and glory.

The City of God Has Towers

The eternal city is called "the city of the living God, the heavenly Jerusalem" (Heb 12:22). Many of the world's leading cities have a skyline, marked by skyscrapers. If that's true of earthly cities, then why would it not also be true of the city of God? It's entirely plausible to suppose that the city of God has a skyline with towering skyscrapers.

Furthermore, I want to suggest that the skyscrapers in the city of God signify the testimonies of outstanding men and women of faith. David observed, "He is the tower of salvation to His king" (2 Sam 22:51). In other words, sometimes God builds a tower of salvation with the lives of His chosen ones.

In speaking of the heavenly Zion, the psalmist invited, "Count her towers" (Ps 48:12). He said that Zion has towers, bulwarks, and palaces that testify to the greatness of God (see Ps 48:12–14). I'm suggesting that Zion's towers are the dwelling places of saints in the New Jerusalem who are inhabiting a towering testimony of God's faithfulness in their lives.

The psalmist told us to walk around the city of God and counts her towers. In other words, he urged us to examine and consider the towering testimonies that God constructed with the lives of faith heroes. Hebrews 11 mentions some of the skyscraper stories of history, embodied in the lives of faithful witnesses such as Abel, Enoch, Noah, Abraham, Sarah, Jacob, Joseph, Moses, Rahab, Samuel, David, and others. We should look at their stories, ponder their significance, and consider what kind of story God is writing with our lives.

Much planning and labor goes into the construction of a skyscraper. If God is building a tower of salvation with the story of your life, therefore, you might identify personally with some of the following observations.

Towers Have Stories

Every skyscraper has its own story. Tour the tower, and the tour guide will tell you the story. She'll tell you what the tower signifies or commemorates, or why it was built, or who it's dedicated to, or what its presence was meant to accomplish. There's a reason the tower was built—that is, there's a *why* behind the *what*. It's too intentional and massive to lack a story.

In the eternal city, there's one skyscraper that towers above all others, and the story behind it is more colossal than any other. Tour that tower, and you'll be told about Calvary. At the cross, God constructed the largest skyscraper of human history. When you count the towers of Zion, Calvary will be *number one*. Those who walk the streets of the New Jerusalem can see that the name of Jesus towers above every other name.

At Calvary, God crafted a story to exalt the name of His Son. Similarly, when He writes a towering story with your life, your witness will bring glory and honor to His name.

If a story is to arrest its audience, it must have a compelling plot. In the same way, for your story to become a towering testimony, it must have a gripping narrative.

Have you thought your storyline is crazy or bizarre? It might feel like that in the moment, but when you get to the other side and look back, you'll be amazed at what God built with your life. You'll realize that the intensity of your storyline, strange as it may have seemed at the time, was actually *necessary* so that your story might become a skyscraper.

Skyscrapers Are Expensive

Skyscrapers are incredibly expensive to build. For starters, they're usually constructed on some of the most expensive real estate of urban centers. Additionally, they have scores of floors, with some of them over one hundred stories high. When you have over one hundred floors in a building, the cost of construction per square foot (in terms of the foundation's imprint) skyrockets exorbitantly.

But once finished, the skyscraper becomes the glory of its city.

Applied to our lives, if God chooses to build a skyscraper with our lives, we'll pay a steep price. Look at the cross as the ultimate example of that truth, where Christ paid the most extravagant price to gain for His Father the greatest glory. Similarly, we'll doubtless pay a sobering price for a towering testimony, but we'll have the dignity of giving glory to the magnificent grace of Jesus.

Towers Are Visible for Miles Around

When I visited Taiwan, I had the privilege of touring Taipei's famous skyscraper, Taipei 101 (so named because it has 101 floors). What an amazing edifice! It reaches 1,667 feet (508 meters) into the sky and, at the time of this writing, ranks the tenth tallest building in the world. The place is a tourist trap. People come from all around the world to stand at its base, admire its height, and then view the city of Taipei from its lofty observation decks.

A skyscraper can't be hidden. There is no structure in Taiwan that comes even close to rivaling Taipei 101's height. It towers far above all its surroundings and can be seen for many miles in all directions.

The same may be true of your story. If God fashions a skyscraper with your life, it'll be visible to many nations and generations.

The psalmist said that when people look at the towers of Zion, they'll say, "This is God, our God forever and ever!" (Ps 48:14). In other words, they'll look at the testimonies of faith heroes and give praise to God: "This is how God works. These stories demonstrate the character and ways of God. They show how good and faithful He is to His chosen ones. When I look at the towering testimonies God has constructed with these saints, my confidence in His goodness becomes unshakable. This God is my God! He's going to be just as faithful in the way He writes my story."

When God builds a towering testimony with your life, no one will be able to keep the story hidden. It'll be visible to multitudes in every direction. When they see what God has built with your life, they'll say, "This is God! This is what He is like!" They won't be talking about *you*, they'll be talking about *Him*.

Towers Are Uncommonly Few

When you consider how many buildings are constructed in the cities of the earth, skyscrapers are comparatively few. Only a few cities in the world have one. That's one reason they stand out so much and draw so much interest. Their rarity makes them a public attraction.

Skyscrapers are rare. Furthermore, each one is unique from every other tower in the world. When the Twin Towers stood in New York City, they were an exception in the sense that the two towers mirrored each other. But in virtually every other instance, each skyscraper has its own unique architecture, design, and height.

The higher the tower, the deeper the footers

In a similar way, the towers of the eternal city are comparatively few and rare. They're few enough that, unlike the sand of the sea, you can *count* them.

What does this mean for our lives? It means that you can ask God to write a one-of-a-kind story with your life. When He constructs towering testimonies, each is singularly different from all others. It's not that your journey is weird or strange (see 1 Pet 4:12), but it certainly is uniquely outstanding.

Towers Take Years to Build

A skyscraper is never a short-term project. A low skyline might go up fairly quickly but not a skyscraper skyline. Generally, the taller the tower, the longer the construction timeline. When erecting a tall one, each phase of the construction seems to take *forever*. Excavation? Takes forever. Pouring the foundation? Takes forever. Erecting the frame and superstructure? Takes forever. Finishing the interior? Takes forever.

The same is true when God is writing a towering story with your life. A short story will produce but a low skyline. But in cases where God is building a towering testimony, it will take years—even decades—from start to finish.

You've probably noticed this already, but God's not writing a short story with your life. Buckle up, this one will take a while.

Towers Require Footers

The higher a building is erected, the deeper its foundation must reach. This is especially true of the skyscrapers of the world. Their footers must, of necessity, go deep enough to support the above-ground architecture.

To go high, you must first go deep. The higher the tower, the deeper the footers.

You'll see this principle in the cross of Christ. At

the cross, God was building the most soaring sky-scraper of eternity. To build that high, God had to go extra deep. That's why the cross was so extraordinarily intense. God had to excavate the heart of Christ to its very depths so that He could erect the tower of our salvation on Mount Calvary. The deepest dig made way for the most prominent pinnacle.

God still works the same way in our lives. When He builds a tower of salvation with our lives (see 2 Sam 22:51), the promised heights will require that He excavate deeply in our lives so the footers can support the tower. The deep dig reveals how high He plans to go with the story.

You can't get a great story out of a pathetic plot; and you can't erect a towering testimony on a shallow bed.

Psalm 92:5 says, "O LORD, how great are Your works! Your thoughts are very deep." Great works require deep thinking. When God plans a great tower, He thinks deeply about the necessary foundation.

Footers require excavation. Excavation, therefore, is the first step in the process of building. Before you can work your way up, you must first work your way down.

Excavation at a construction site is rigorous and invasive. The same is true in our lives personally. When God chooses to build a skyscraper witness with our lives, He starts by excavating our hearts in a way that is invasive, challenging, and unsettling to us. In order to make room for the footers, He'll remove old foundations that seemed to serve our previous structures adequately. But the old foundations won't support the new structures God plans to build into our lives. To support the new tower, the old foundations will need to be removed, and then the excavations of our heart driven even deeper.

The depth and rigor of this kind of excavation in our hearts by the Holy Spirit can be so intense that the only thing that pulls us through is the assurance that the deep digging will be followed by upward construction. Carried by hope in His goodness, we don't resist or complain about the deep dig; rather, we trust in the wisdom of our Master Craftsman.

Here's the point I'm underscoring: To build an adequate foundation in your life, the excavation process is *necessary*. The tower can only go as high as the footers go deep.

For the towering testimony God is writing with your life, you have actually *needed* this excavation.

8

EVEN MORE BENEFITS OF TRIALS

By now, you're getting the point of this book. As difficult as trials are, sometimes we need them in our lives.

If we respond properly to them, the benefits are fantastic. Trials arrest our attention and fix our focus on Jesus. They make us more zealous to repent and obey. They help us jettison the distractions and temptations that thwart our progress. They drive us into God for fresh revelation. They accelerate our growth curve and help us change into the image of Christ. They get us listening to God more closely. They move us into intimacy with God, where we develop an abiding relationship with Christ and become more fruitful than ever. And the list goes on.

Once we've overcome, we'll probably say, "I needed that trial." As the psalmist said, "It is good for me that I have been afflicted, that I may learn Your statutes" (Ps 119:71).

The Bible is chock full of stories illustrating the

necessity of trials. Once you start looking for it, you see this truth *everywhere* in Scripture. In this chapter, follow with me as I mention seven such stories in succinct, rapid-fire succession.

Israel in Babylon

The nation of Israel was exiled to Babylon for seventy years, and I'm persuaded they *needed* the captivity in Babylon. God used the Babylonian captivity to extract idolatry from the hearts of His people. The captivity didn't make them perfect, but when they returned home from Babylon, they left their idols behind.

Idolatry had been a national plague for Israel for hundreds of years, but the captivity cauterized something within them. The nation of Israel never returned to the kinds of idolatry that had persisted throughout their pre-captivity years. That purging helped to prepare the nation for the coming of their Messiah.

As difficult as it was, they *needed* the seventy-year exile.

Hannah's Heartache

Hannah was a young wife in the Bible who was desperate for a baby. But alas, she was barren. It might sound harsh to say it so bluntly, but Hannah actually *needed* her barrenness. Why? Because barrenness was the pivotal backdrop against which one of the most seminal stories of the Bible was written.

The book of 1 Samuel opens with the story of Hannah's relentless longing. All she wanted was a son, and even though her husband tried to comfort her with food and with his affections, he could do little to assuage her sorrow.

Desperate for a baby, Hannah went to the Lord's tabernacle in Shiloh to pray. "Give me a son! I've got to have a son!" As her soul reached for God, her prayers turned dangerous. She began to say things to God that no woman would ordinarily say.

"God, give me a son! If You'll give me a son, I'll— God, if You'll give me a son, I'll—I'll—*give him back to You!*" (see 1 Sam 1:11).

God's response was basically, "Done! That's the desperate prayer I've been waiting to hear. It's a deal!"

No wife with normal maternal instincts wants to give up her baby. When Hannah offered to give him up, this was an unnatural prayer. It was a desperate prayer. It was the kind of dangerous praying that captures heaven's attention.

Much was at stake, and God needed to raise up a Samuel for Himself. It was time to transition the nation from the era of the judges to the era of the kings. A powerful prophet was needed to guide the nation through such a tumultuous and significant transition. When Hannah prayed her dangerous prayer, God gave her Samuel—the prophet who anointed Saul to be Israel's first king.

When Hannah gave birth to Samuel and then gave him back to the Lord, Samuel grew up in the tabernacle under the care of Eli the priest. Reared in the courts of the Lord, Samuel learned to hear the voice of God and grew into a mighty prophet.

How did God get His Samuel? By making a woman barren. As grievous as the trial was to Hannah, it was actually *necessary* in order for her to give birth to Samuel.

David's Cave

For around ten years, Saul hunted David in order to kill him. The cave of Adullam came to represent David's years of hiding from Saul because it was such a dank haunt, and he spent so much time there. Being hunted by Saul was a trial that vexed David's soul grievously, but yet I want to suggest that he *needed* the cave of Adullam in his life. Why? Let me explain.

God's destiny for David was that he eventually make his way to the high hills of the kingdom—the high hills of prophetic revelation and spiritual authority in answered prayer. But David would have to be prepared for such heights. That's why God took him first through the valley of the shadow of death (see Ps 23:4). The valley is the place where God prepares us for the mountain. He trains our feet in the valley so we can walk the high hills of the kingdom.

David wrote, "He makes my feet like the feet

of deer, and sets me on my high places" (Ps 18:33). David meant that God prepared his feet in the valley of his wilderness years so that he could safely tread the high places of his spiritual inheritance in his later years. Habakkuk expressed it this way: "He will make my feet like deer's feet, and He will make me walk on my high hills" (Hab 3:19).

The feet of deer are especially designed to help them navigate sheer slopes without slipping or injuring themselves. If you should ever watch a nature film of deer navigating steep slopes, you'll be amazed at how sure-footed they are on dangerous precipices.

The high places of the kingdom—places of great conquest and lofty revelation—are marked by high escarpments and steep ravines. A fall on the high places of grace can be devastating. Therefore, before God promotes His Davids to the high places, He prepares their feet in the valley.

A valley season indicates that God is *for* you. He's training you for the lofty call on your life.

David's son, Solomon, inherited his father's throne, and both of them walked the high places of the kingdom. Both of them had uncommon revelation, wisdom, and divine favor. But there was one huge difference between David and Solomon: David endured safely in truth, while Solomon took a catastrophic fall to idolatry.

What was the cause for this great difference

between them? Answer: *Solomon had no cave of Adullam.* Solomon was given the mountain without the training of the valley and, consequently, took a devastating fall on the mountain's precipices.

God loves you too much to give you the promotion without the pruning. Like David, you also will *need* your feet to be trained in the valley so that you can safely walk your high hills without becoming a spiritual casualty.

The Prodigal Son

> *God loves you too much to give you the promotion without the pruning*

In Jesus' famous parable, the prodigal son actually *needed* the famine that hit the land (see Luke 15:11–32). The famine made him hungry, hunger brought him to his senses, and clear thinking led him back to his father. Without the famine, who knows how long the wayward son might have continued to wander in a fruitless path.

The famine was a grievous trial, but heaven sent it because God knew the prodigal son actually *needed* the famine to get his life back in order.

The *God of the Famine* still sends famines into our lives at strategic times when necessary.

The Church at Jerusalem

After Jesus ascended to heaven, a powerful revival broke out in Jerusalem, and thousands of Jews came into the faith. The sense of community, purpose, power, and momentum was galvanizing and magnetic. A spirit of repentance rested on the people, and signs and wonders were performed continually. Everybody wanted to be in Jerusalem to enjoy the warmth of the revival fires.

But Jesus didn't want them to stay in Jerusalem. He had given them a commission to take the gospel to the nations (see Matt 28:19–20). Instead of launching out on their commission, however, they were gathered together in Jerusalem in delightful joy and fellowship. The outpouring of the Spirit was just too good, and nobody wanted to leave.

How would God dislodge them and send them to the nations? He selected persecution as His tool of choice. He allowed a great persecution to arise against the church in Jerusalem, and the persecution caused the believers to scatter everywhere (see Acts 8:1).

The persecution was extremely distressful for the believers. They were losing homesteads and family inheritances. Uprooted from all that was familiar, they were forced to find other places to live. To the believers, the persecution gutted them of their livelihoods;

but to God, it helped them take the gospel everywhere they went. From God's perspective, the persecution was *necessary*.

The church needed the persecution to thrust
them forth from the comforts of Jerusalem to the re-
gions beyond. In a similar way, sometimes we actually
need persecution.

Paul's Thorn

I want to suggest that Paul needed his thorn in
the flesh. Why? Well, he himself gave this explanation:

> *And lest I should be exalted above measure by*
> *the abundance of the revelations, a thorn in the*
> *flesh was given to me, a messenger of Satan*
> *to buffet me, lest I be exalted above measure*
> *(2 Cor 12:7).*

When God graces someone with unusual revelation, crowds are wowed and impressed. They gather
eagerly to hear the exceptional insight and unique
understanding.

Paul had been graced by the Lord Jesus in this
way. God had given him uncommon revelation and
insight into the gospel of grace, and crowds were always gathering to hear those mysteries of the gospel.
Moved deeply by Paul's preaching, the people were
tempted to get their eyes on Paul and think more
highly of him than they ought.

That's why God gave Paul his thorn in the flesh. It was a demonic affliction in his body that made him appear weak and pitiful in the sight of people. Such a pitiful sight would help people keep their focus on Jesus rather than getting impressed with Paul.

To remain humble in the eyes of people, Paul *needed* that thorn.

Pruned Branches

Some of the highest truths Jesus spoke are recorded in John 15. Here's how the chapter starts:

> *I am the true vine, and My Father is the vinedresser. Every branch in Me that does not bear fruit He takes away; and every branch that bears fruit He prunes, that it may bear more fruit (John 15:1–2).*

We're His branches, and we bear fruit by abiding in Him. When the life of Christ flows into our lives, we naturally bear fruit to God. One of the great goals of our lives is to become increasingly fruitful in the kingdom.

The Father helps us become more fruitful by pruning us. Although pruning is an unpleasant experience for the branch, the farmer will still prune because he knows that pruning is *necessary* if a branch is to be fruitful in the next season.

In a growing season, a vine will produce fifty or

more new canes. If those canes aren't pruned back but left to remain into the next season, the root won't be able to support all those branches. In the following season, the fruit will be sparse, small, and not sweet enough for wine. In other words, the harvest will be useless. Pruning, therefore, is a necessary kindness.

As branches joined to Christ, we need the trial of pruning if we're to be fruitful.

How many ways can we say it? Sometimes we need trials.

Jesus's Battle

We started this book with our primary verse:

"Thus it is written, and thus it was necessary for the Christ to suffer and to rise from the dead the third day" (Luke 24:46).

Jesus said that His sufferings on the cross were necessary. One reason the cross was necessary was so that Jesus could lay a blow to His adversary's head. Let me explain.

Back in the garden of Eden, the Father had predicted Jesus would do this. After Adam and Eve fell to sin, the Father told Satan that Jesus would bruise his head:

He shall bruise your head, and you shall bruise His heel (Gen 3:15).

The Father was speaking to Satan about the cross.

Anticipating what would happen several millennia later at the cross, God predicted that Satan would crush Jesus's heel, and Jesus would crush Satan's head. In the struggle, both parties would sustain a blow. Satan's blow would be glancing, but Jesus's blow would be devastating.

When Jesus hung on the cross, with nails driven through His heels, it didn't *feel* like a mere bruising of His heel; it felt like His entire being was being crushed, particle by particle—because it was.

But if we were to talk to Jesus today about His cross, He would speak about it from an eternal perspective. He might say something like, "Wow, that was intense, I really took it in the heel. But my adversary has been bloodied in the head!"

When we're in a fiery trial, our experience is much the same. In the vortex of the trial, we might feel like we're being pulled apart molecule by molecule—because we probably are. But if we'll endure in faith, one day we'll see our trial from a very different perspective—from God's eternal perspective.

There's a day coming when you will look back at the trial that's crushing you today, and despise the pain you're in right now. Why? Because in contrast to the hit you took, your adversary will have suffered a much greater blow. You'll probably say something like, "Wow, that was intense, I really took it in the heel. But my adversary has been bloodied in the head!"

Yes, I'm suggesting that God wants to use your trial to bloody the head of your adversary. By the time it's done, you will do more damage to your enemy than if the trial had never happened. Just as Satan deeply regrets taking on Jesus at the cross, may he also regret the day he took you on.

Do you want to lay a blow to the head of your adversary? Ask Jesus to show you how. He's real good at spiritual warfare, and He's willing to take you on as His apprentice. Ask Him how He leveled the devil with a knockout punch at the cross. If you come in humility, He'll make of you a mighty warrior and show you how to lay a blow to the head of your adversary.

Jesus had to do the cross. Why? So He could land a knockout punch to the head of His adversary. Do you also want to wound the head of your adversary? If yes, then this fiery trial you're enduring is probably *necessary*. You'll take it in the heel, but your adversary will take it in the head.

9

THE RESURRECTION WAS ALSO NECESSARY

For one last time, let's return to our theme verse. Jesus said:

Thus it is written, and thus it was necessary for the Christ to suffer and to rise from the dead the third day (Luke 24:46).

As a reminder, this was Jesus—after the resurrection—debriefing with His disciples about the cross. Now that He was risen, what did He have to say about His sufferings? Basically just one thing: "The cross was *necessary*."

Knowing that His sufferings were necessary, Jesus was able to worship His Father on the cross. How do we know He worshiped on the cross? Well, the gospel writers don't include this in their accounts of the crucifixion. To see Jesus worshiping on the cross, you have to go back to the writings of David.

In Psalm 22, David entered prophetically into the anguish of the crucifixion, identified with Christ's sufferings, and cried out to God with words that Jesus

Himself later quoted while hanging on the cross:

> *My God, My God, why have You forsaken Me?*
> *Why are You so far from helping Me, and from*
> *the words of My groaning? ...But You are holy,*
> *enthroned in the praises of Israel (Ps 22:1, 3).*

Psalm 22 in its entirety is a cross psalm. And in verse three, David represented Jesus saying to His Father, "You are holy." David helped us see that Jesus, in the vortex of His agony on the cross, worshiped His Father.

By saying "You are holy" to His Father, Jesus was essentially saying, "You are perfect. Your leadership in My life is brilliant. I have no accusation against You, but only praise for Your goodness in My life. You are compassionate, tender, merciful, kind, benevolent, and gracious. You are leading Me in the paths of righteousness. You are holy."

There are two ways you can worship God in your trial. On the one hand, you can say things like, "You are kind. You are tender. You're compassionate and merciful, gracious, dependable, unchanging, unrivaled, unique, beautiful, righteous, just, strong, mighty, omnipotent, omniscient, omnipresent, wise, discerning, healing, delivering, saving, helping, redeeming, restoring, carrying, caring, humble, longsuffering, good, true, bright, fiery, jealous, wrathful, judging, vengeful, enlightening, unstoppable, transcendent, immanent, patient, faithful, brilliant, excellent, enduring, unpredictable, living, enlivening, pure, undefiled, blameless, able, equitable, glorious, majestic, eternal, immortal, invisible, burning, jealous, loving, enthroned, militant, victorious, conquering, forgiving, cleansing, immovable, unshakable, wonderful, unsearchable, and unfathomable."

Or, on the other hand, to say all of that at once, you can simply say, "You are holy." *Holy* is all His glorious attributes bound up in one sublime word.

Jesus had no accusation against His Father, even though His Father was killing Him. But it wasn't just an absence of accusation that characterized Christ's attitude; He actually *dignified* His Father's crushing. "You've forsaken Me, but You're perfect in all Your ways. The way You're handling Me right now is right, wise, and good. You are holy!"

Just as the cross was necessary, so was the resurrection

Let me be honest for a moment about my own struggle. I have suffered for decades (at the time of this writing) in a fiery trial, and the Lord has promised to deliver me. However, His deliverance has not yet come. And as I've waited for my miracle, I have struggled to worship Him for this trial. I could worship Him *in* the trial, but I didn't know how to worship Him *for* the trial. Why not? I'll try to explain.

God has promised to heal and deliver me, and I

hold His promise as one of the most cherished treasures of my life. I'll never let go His promise! I didn't
know, though, how I could maintain my hold on His
promise and at the same time thank Him for my trial.
It seemed to me that if I were to thank and praise Him
for this trial, that I'd have to let go my promise of deliverance. If I worship Him *for* the trial, am I not implicitly
accepting it as my permanent lot in life? But I *can't* ac-
cept this trial as my permanent lot in life because I've
got too many promises from Him of His assured deliverance. Therefore, for years I struggled to worship and
thank Him for my trial.

But then I took a second look at Luke 24:46. Here,
I'll quote it again:

> *Thus it is written, and thus it was necessary for
> the Christ to suffer and to rise from the dead the
> third day (Luke 24:46).*

Jesus said His cross was necessary, but that wasn't the
end of the sentence. He then went on to say that His
resurrection was *also* necessary. Just as His cross was
necessary, so was His resurrection. Just as His trial was
necessary, so was His deliverance.

The same is true for both you and me. *Just as
this trial has been necessary in your life, so too is your
resurrection.*

The cross was never intended to be the last chapter in your story. The cross is *wonderful*, but by itself

insufficient; crucifixion must be followed by resurrection. The story is never complete until it's graced with the capstone of resurrection.

Your resurrection is *essential!* Therefore, just as Jesus worshiped His Father in the middle of His agony, so can you. The nails are still in your hands and feet, but even so, you can lift your eyes to your Beloved and say, "You are holy. You are good. You are true. You are leading me perfectly in the paths of righteousness. I worship You because I have needed this trial, and I worship You because You're going to raise me up again."

Yes, your trial has been necessary; but even better than that, *your resurrection is also necessary!*

May you be granted eyes of faith to see God's perspective on your trial. Just as Jesus's cross was necessary, your fiery trial has been necessary. It's proving the authenticity of your faith and producing faith that is much more precious than gold. He's poured you from vessel to vessel in order to refresh your fragrance. The storm has made your branches more flexible so you can support the fruit of your next season. Through the stressful drought, He's produced a vintage wine with your life. He's erecting a towering testimony with your story. He's training your feet in the valley so you can walk your high hills. And He'll finish the story by raising you up.

May you lay a blow to the head of your adversary. Amen!

BOOKS BY BOB SORGE

Prayer

Secrets of the Secret Place (paperback & hardcover)
Secrets of the Secret Place: Companion Study Guide
Secrets of the Secret Place: Leader's Manual
Reset: 20 Ways to a Consistent Prayer Life
Unrelenting Prayer
Illegal Prayers
Power of the Blood
Minute Meditations

Worship

*Exploring Worship: A Practical Guide to Praise and
    Worship*
Exploring Worship Workbook & Discussion Guide
Glory: When Heaven Invades Earth
Following The River: A Vision for Corporate Worship
Next Wave: Worship in a New Era

Enduring Faith

In His Face
The Fire Of Delayed Answers
The Fire Of God's Love
*Pain, Perplexity, & Promotion: A Prophetic Interpretation
    of the Book of Job*
Opened From the Inside: Taking the Stronghold of Zion
God's Still Writing Your Story
The Chastening of the Lord: The Forgotten Doctrine

The Cross: Never Too Dead for Resurrection
It's Not a Tomb It's a Womb
Sometimes We Need Trials

Leadership
Dealing With the Rejection and Praise of Man
Envy: The Enemy Within
Loyalty: The Reach Of The Noble Heart
It's Not Business It's Personal
A Covenant With My Eyes
Stuck: Help for the Troubled Home

For info on each title, go to oasishouse.com
Call Oasis House at 816-767-8880

Bob's books are also available at:
    christianbook.com
    amazon.com
    Kindle, iBooks, Nook, Google Play
    Audible

Stay connected with Bob at:
    YouTube.com/bobsorge
    Facebook.com/BobSorgeMinistry
    Blog: bobsorge.com
    Instagram: bob.sorge
    Twitter.com/BOBSORGE